D1924957

—— T H E ——
McGRAW-HILL
36-Hour Course

OPERATIONS
MANAGEMENT

Other books in The McGraw-Hill 36-Hour Course series:

THE
McGRAW-HILL
36-Hour Course

OPERATIONS MANAGEMENT

Linda L. Brennan, Ph.D.

RETIRÉ DE LA COLLECTION UNIVERSELLE
Bibliothèque et Archives nationales du Québec

New York Chicago San Francisco Lisbon London Madrid Mexico City
Milan New Delhi San Juan Seoul Singapore Sydney Toronto

The McGraw·Hill Companies

Copyright © 2011 by Linda Brennan. All rights reserved. Printed in the United States of America. Except as permitted under the United States Copyright Act of 1976, no part of this publication may be reproduced or distributed in any form or by any means, or stored in a database or retrieval system, without the prior written permission of the publisher.

1 2 3 4 5 6 7 8 9 10 11 12 13 14 15 WFR/WFR 1 9 8 7 6 5 4 3 2 1 0

ISBN   978-0-07-174383-9
MHID   0-07-174383-9

This publication is designed to provide accurate and authoritative information in regard to the subject matter covered. It is sold with the understanding that neither the author nor the publisher is engaged in rendering legal, accounting, securities trading, or other professional services. If legal advice or other expert assistance is required, the services of a competent professional person should be sought.
> —From a Declaration of Principles Jointly Adopted by a Committee of the
> American Bar Association and a Committee of Publishers and Associations

Trademarks: McGraw-Hill, the McGraw-Hill Publishing logo, 36-Hour Course, and related trade dress are trademarks or registered trademarks of The McGraw-Hill Companies and/or its affiliates in the United States and other countries and may not be used without written permission. All other trademarks are the property of their respective owners. The McGraw-Hill Companies is not associated with any product or vendor mentioned in this book.

Figures 4-1, 4-3, 4-4, 5-1, 5-2, 6-1, 6-2, 7-1, 7-2, 8-1, 8-2, 8-3, 8-4a, 8-4b, 8-5, 10-2, 10-3, 11-1, and 12-1 by Glyph International.

McGraw-Hill books are available at special quantity discounts to use as premiums and sales promotions or for use in corporate training programs. To contact a representative, please e-mail us at bulksales@mcgraw-hill.com.

This book is printed on acid-free paper.

*This book is dedicated to Mudge,
my very large chocolate lab, who parked himself
behind my desk chair whenever I sat down to write—
and would not let me out until my job was done.*

CONTENTS

PREFACE

I first started teaching operations management to M.B.A. students in 1995. Despite trying many different textbooks and reading packets since then, I have yet to find a book that my students and I think is useful, much less interesting. The texts inevitably cover an overly broad range of topics and present superficial versions of management science techniques that students are unlikely to remember (or use) in the workplace.

What is needed is an enduring framework by which to evaluate operations, identify opportunities to improve them, implement changes, and measure outcomes—what I think of as "managing for results." I believe this framework should be applicable at the organizational, team, and individual levels of performance—whether in a manufacturing plant, a services sector, a government department, or a personal life. You will find this philosophy undergirds the entire book and is reflected in its organization.

The first three chapters are devoted to building an understanding of the importance and scope of operations management, an appreciation for a systems perspective and scientific thinking, and a foundation in performance measurement. As the old adage goes, "If you give a man a fish, he eats for a day; if you teach a man to fish, he eats for life." Once you have this basic knowledge, you can learn how to manage operations, regardless of the context (or body of water).

Next we explore key operations management initiatives that involve an entire organization. New product and services development, quality programs, and technological applications are organization-wide efforts that can have a profound impact on operational effectiveness. These topics, with relevant techniques, are covered in Chapters 4 through 6.

In Chapters 7 and 8, we turn our focus from the organization as a whole to processes. First we examine process effectiveness—consistently adding value while eliminating waste and focusing on throughout. Then we tackle process quality, using statistical thinking to monitor process variability.

Chapters 9, 10, and 11 focus on individual projects, from definition and planning to scheduling and control. A process in and of itself, project management is the most important tool in an operations manager's toolkit. Any work done to improve an operation's performance will be achieved through specific projects.

The last chapter serves as a summary by challenging you to apply what you have learned about operations management to your own personal performance, or an operation of one. You may consider ways in which to be more competitive in the workforce, more efficient in your daily activities, less inclined to procrastinate, or more intentional about your desired results.

To find the answers to the end-of-chapter review questions and to take the final exam, visit 36hourbooks.com.

Whether you are concerned with operations at the organizational, process, project, or personal level, I hope that you will find this book useful and the material enduring. In the spirit of continuous improvement, I welcome your comments, questions, suggestions, and experiences. Let me hear from you at LLBrennanBooks@Cox.net.

ACKNOWLEDGMENTS

Not only is the content of this course book different from that of your typical operations management textbook, the delivery of that content is also unconventional. The conversational tone and occasional bits of humor are deliberate. My intent is to make the material engaging and readable, even (dare I say?) interesting.

To the extent that I have succeeded is largely based on the devotion of my wonderful husband. As a business practitioner, he has a strong sense of smell for "academic gloss" and a wonderful attention to detail. He also has a great sense of humor and could not have been more supportive of this project. I am so thankful that I walked into the wrong bathroom at IBM and found him there all those years ago.

I must also thank our son. First, you have to love a teenager who understands throughput! Also, when I first started this book, I was apparently very interruptible. After I put a sign on the door saying, "Do not disturb unless you are bleeding or choking," he got the hint. (The kid is very smart.) He and my husband bless me every day.

So does my mother, who was full of encouragement. Turtles remind me to be steadfast and persist, so Mom made sure I had turtles. In my home office, campus office, sitting room, screened porch—anywhere I might even *think* about the book.

I have also been blessed with some marvelous mentors in this season of my career. Gerry, Skip, and Victoria are all published authors who encouraged me on this journey. I am thankful for their guidance and their friendship.

Finally, I want to thank the editorial team at McGraw-Hill. Whirlwinds of efficiency, they definitely know how to manage for results!

1

MANAGING FOR RESULTS

If you don't know where you're going, it doesn't
much matter how you get there.
—THE CHESHIRE CAT (PARAPHRASED FROM
ALICE IN WONDERLAND BY LEWIS CARROLL)

When you think about operations, what picture comes to mind? If you're like most people, you think of a manufacturing plant or assembly line. Occasionally, I will have a student who relates it to the context of surgery, as in "I'm having an operation to remove a tumor tomorrow."
While none of these ideas is wrong, the correct answer is much broader. Operations consist of whatever an organization does to make inputs become outputs. It's that simple. Really. Whether the organization is a service company, a government agency, a not-for-profit entity, or a publicly traded corporation, it obtains inputs. Operations transform these inputs by adding value to them (and sometimes wasted effort) and make them available to others as outputs. Operations management is about managing for results—that is, desired outputs.

After completing this chapter, you should be able to do the following:

- Describe an operation as a *transformation* system
- Explain the importance of operations management
- Recognize opportunities for operational improvements
- Identify sources of *competitive advantage* in an operation

Throughout this book, you will find a practical, commonsense approach to managing for results. Common sense is logical, has an intuitive appeal, and is clear when you think about it. There is a practical connotation to common sense. Unfortunately, as the architect Frank Lloyd Wright noted, "There is nothing more uncommon than common sense."

Not sure you agree? Consider the case of the rolling suitcase. The idea is that the case is too heavy to carry through the airport, so you pull it on wheels. Yet somehow you are expected to lift it into an overhead compartment to stow it away. (Not to mention that the people who pushed ahead of you to get on the plane first took more than their allotted amount of overhead space.) Why not have bench seats with storage underneath? No one would get hurt, and all those bags wouldn't impinge on your space. Isn't that common sense?

Why do we have daylight savings time in fully electrified countries? Why do we have a nine-month school year when children are no longer needed to work in the fields during the summer? Why do we still teach cursive writing in primary education when very little is handwritten anymore? Because we have done things this way for as long as anyone remembers.

Operations are like that. You can do something over and over, because that is how you have always done it, and you can make operations very complex. Or you can use basic principles that are memorable and have an intuitive appeal to cover most situations. Once you understand these principles, they will seem like common sense. This is the essence of the 36-hour course in operations management.

OPERATIONS AS A TRANSFORMATION FUNCTION

Inputs can come in conventional forms as direct labor, direct materials, and other direct costs. Inputs can also be capital items that are not consumed in the operation. The idea of capital as cash wealth invested for a specific purpose (such as technology, equipment, and land) has broadened to include human capital (labor), intellectual capital (knowledge), and social capital (reputation, brand equity, customer loyalty, and so on).

Outputs can be categorized in several different ways. Generally we think in terms of goods or services, but often outputs are a combination of both, on a continuum from mostly service to mostly goods. On one end of the spectrum (mostly service) is an airplane ticket that represents a transportation service; in addition to the service, you may receive a drink and possibly a meal as goods. The ticket itself is a *facilitating good*, something that enables you to receive the service. On the other end of the spectrum is the purchase of a new refrigerator. You are buying the product as well as the delivery service that will enable you to use the product in your home.

Outputs can also be classified as tangible or intangible, in the sense that something is tangible if it can be perceived by touch. Clearly, products are tangible. Production waste is tangible. Facilitating goods are tangible. Even some services—such as a haircut, car wash, or packing/moving service—are tangible. Intangible outputs tend to be emotional or experiential results such as satisfaction, relaxation, convenience, and ambience.

As I write this, I am sitting in a Starbucks, sipping a cappuccino, and biding my time between meetings. My drink is a tangible product. The chair in which I am sitting is a facilitating good that enables me to enjoy the intangible ambience. I am also enjoying the convenience of a comfortable place to work before my next meeting, which is across town from my office.

To create any kind of output, an organization transforms inputs. There are four elemental transformation functions: alter, inspect, store, and transport.[1] They are applicable whether the output is a good, a service, or a combination of the two. An organization adds value to its inputs by performing some combination of these functions. If it does not add value, then why would a customer purchase that organization's output instead of purchasing the inputs directly?

In my Starbucks illustration, the milk and coffee have been altered: the milk has been steamed and frothed, and the coffee beans were ground, tamped, and expressed. Before serving it to me, the barista inspected the drink. The drink may also be considered as a product bundled with a service. Since I choose to stay at the store, Starbucks is also providing me with a storage service (for my person), a place to wait while I consume my beverage.

The retail products available at Starbucks, such as bulk coffee, mugs, and coffee machines, are all goods that can be purchased elsewhere. Since Starbucks has transformed them by transporting the products to this location and storing them on the display shelves, they have added value to them by providing convenient accessibility and the implied endorsement of being good enough to make Starbucks coffee. The company has also altered the bulk coffee by adding the Starbucks logo and packaging. This adds the social capital of branding to the inputs and provides an assurance of quality as an intangible output.

Operations are at the core of any enterprise. The effective management of operations is therefore one of the most critical success factors for an organization.

OPERATIONS AS A COMPETITIVE ADVANTAGE

Often, executives and managers outside of the operational function view it as the routine (and possibly uninteresting) part of the organization. This may be true, but it is not the complete picture. I call this "elevator vision." Elevators are part of a building that you really only notice when they don't work. In the same way, when operations are viewed as routine, they only receive significant management attention when there is a problem.

That is one of the reasons that thinking of operations as a transformation function is foundational to our course. This perspective emphasizes results and encourages management to focus on where the value is added in the transformation process. Shifting perspectives in this way can have a significant impact on business strategy.

There are innumerable taxonomies, diagrams, and academic frameworks for strategic management. For our purposes, suffice it to say that something is "strategic" when it creates or sustains a competitive advantage. By viewing operations as processes that add value to inputs through a transformation that results in outputs, you can more easily identify ways in which operations management can be a source of competitive advantage.

How can operations help to make an organization more competitive? Put simply, an operation provides a competitive advantage by delivering products and services better, faster, and/or cheaper than the competition. That's common sense! *Better* comes from higher quality. *Faster* is achieved by being more responsive and flexible. *Cheaper* is the result of reducing costs. These are general terms, of course; we will delve more deeply into these ideas in subsequent chapters. For now, consider the following "*value matrix*" and how it might inform strategic planning by applying better/faster/cheaper to the transformation function. (See Table 1-1.) This is a general approach that can help managers articulate the importance of operational

Table 1-1 The Value Matrix—General Approach

Source of Value	Inputs	Transformations	Outputs
Better?	How can obtaining or retaining high-quality inputs make a difference?	Can we add more value as we alter, inspect, transport, and store?	How can we deliver hard-to-replicate outputs?
Faster?	Can our requirements be changed to make us more flexible?	Could different approaches streamline operations?	How can we increase our responsiveness?
Cheaper?	How can we reduce the costs of obtaining inputs?	Where are we wasting resources by not adding value?	How can we find salable uses of by-products?

considerations in the overall business strategy. Being competitive takes a lot more than a good marketing strategy; companies are expected to execute and deliver to earn customer loyalty.

Long recognized for its cost competitiveness, Wal-Mart has made a strategic move to further reduce costs and provide faster service. Vying directly against what is seen as Amazon.com's weakness, the costs and delays of shipping online purchases to customers, Walmart.com customers can have their orders shipped free of charge to a local Wal-Mart and pick up their purchases at special service desks.[2] This operation leverages the existing transportation costs of Wal-Mart stores, encourages online customers to come to the stores, and presumably delivers what the customers want faster and cheaper.

When I was a child, I remember enjoying trips to the hardware store with my father, being fascinated by all the stuff the local shop owner managed to cram into a relatively small retail space. You don't find many such stores since the advent of "big box" retailers (Home Depot, Lowe's, Wal-Mart, and so on). Interestingly, though, our metropolitan area has a local hardware store that seems to be able to compete successfully against the bigger retailers. Why? Well, if we examine the situation in terms of better/faster/cheaper, the local store has some clear advantages, as shown in Table 1-2. The local store is part of a franchised chain, which provides some economies of scale that enable the owner to leverage the chain's buying power when purchasing products for sale. He is also more technologically advanced

Table 1-2　A Value Matrix Example

Source of Value	Inputs	Transformations	Outputs
Better?	Knowledgeable staff is readily available to answer questions or offer suggestions.	With staff assistance, customers are more likely to get what they need in one trip.	The in-store consultation makes it more likely the project will be completed successfully.
Faster?	The franchise's inventory systems make restocking more efficient.	A convenient store location and small parking lot make it easier to get in and out.	A customer database streamlines the checkout process.
Cheaper?	As a franchise, the small store can enjoy some economies of scale.	Better compensation and working conditions keep employee turnover low.	Customers are willing to pay more for the bundle of goods and services.

than he might have been as a totally independent operator, because he uses the franchise's information systems (such as inventory control, a customer database, and the bar code scanner).

The key difference in his strategy, though, is the caliber of employees he hires. They are typically experienced problem solvers who enjoy helping others and take pride in their work; often, they are retired from other professions. Another notable difference is in the location of the stores; all three sites he owns are in less congested commercial areas, away from the big chains and more convenient to residential customers.

A prudent business leader understands that the business's value proposition must be distinctive, understood, and feasible. Such a view integrates the domains of operations management, sales/marketing, and finance/accounting. A well-funded business with a sizzling advertising campaign will not last without strong execution. Alternatively, you can have a very effective operational system, but if the awareness of or accessibility to your goods and services is low, you will fail. In the same way, you may have an incredible idea for the "next great thing" and a fabulous promotion plan to get the word out, but if you cannot afford to do any of it, you will still fail. It takes management and coordination of all three domains. Do not settle for routine operations to focus on the other two aspects. A competitive organization is continuously improving its results and achieving a strong balance.

TECHNIQUE: IDENTIFYING SOURCES OF COMPETITIVE ADVANTAGE

We have seen how examining the transformation function of a business can provide a systematic basis to identify its competitive advantages in terms of offering better, faster, and/or cheaper results. An alternative technique for identifying sources of competitive advantage is known as the *resource-based view* (*RBV*) of the firm. First suggested by Wernerfelt, the RBV perspective enables a firm to evaluate existing resources—both tangible and intangible—and determine which to exploit, which to develop, and which to acquire.[3] Lamenting at how infrequently executives were taking the time to consider such matters, Kiernan argued that identifying and protecting an organization's sources of competitive advantage should be common sense.[4]

Building on this perspective, Barney advanced a framework that can be used to evaluate resources and capabilities in terms of value, rareness, inimitability, and organization (*VRIO*).[5] Competitive advantage is achieved through the organized leverage of valuable resources and is sustained by the rareness and inimitability of the resources. More specifically, a firm's resources are valuable when they can be used to exploit opportunities and/or neutralize threats. Property is a tangible resource that is often considered valuable. Brand equity might be a valuable intangible resource.

When few or none of the competing firms have a comparable capability, then it is considered rare. The location of an oceanfront hotel resort might be considered rare. The worldwide recognition of the Coca-Cola trademark is rare.

A resource is inimitable if it creates a disadvantage for competitors and is difficult or impossible for them to attain. A capability may be difficult to imitate because of its path dependency, meaning it was accumulated over time. The "magic" of Disney is hard for others to imitate because of its unusual history, starting with cartoons, moving into feature films, commercializing characters, and building theme parks.

Inimitability may result because it is unclear to competitors how this capability was created (known as "causal ambiguity"), as in the case of Dell Computer's material handling technologies. Or it may be socially complex in a way that is hard to copy, as when key personalities or a distinctive corporate culture are in play—consider Chick-fil-A or Southwest Airlines.

Lastly, a firm is organized when it is prepared to leverage the resource's potential for competitive advantage. If this element is missing, the competitive advantage will evaporate. A classic example is the graphical user interface (GUI) that was developed at Xerox's Palo Alto Research Center (PARC). Unprepared to commercialize the GUI, the organization sold the capability to Steve Jobs for use at Apple. The rest, as they say, is history.

The VRIO model is a practical technique for identifying sources of competitive advantage across an organization, vis-à-vis the competition. In terms of operations management, a VRIO analysis can raise "elevator vision" (bad pun, I know) to examine how operational resources might contribute to the firm's competitive advantage. Rather than holding the organization back or simply being as good as the competition, operations can take a more strategic role and become the best in the industry or even redefine the industry's basis of competition.[6]

For example, when a drug company holds a patent for a new treatment technology, that patent is a valuable resource. If it is also rare, in that there are no other efficacious methods of treatment, the company has an even greater competitive advantage. For the duration of the patent, competitors are unable to imitate the treatment; so for the drug company to use this competitive advantage it must be organized in a way that stimulates demand and provides adequate supply. High-quality, efficient operations are a critical success factor.

One company renowned for its operational excellence is Insight Enterprises. In 2009, Insight received the annual Operational Excellence Award from Microsoft Corporation for the fifth time.[7] Reviewing the company's website, Insight.com, might provide some indication of how a resource-based view of the firm can lead to operational excellence. Founded in 1988, the company ranks in the Fortune 500 and describes itself as "offering software and licensing services globally . . . in addition [to] hardware and value added services . . ."

It's not hard to imagine that, while it grew as a licensed software distributor, Insight noted that there was a larger piece of the information technology (IT) business to win, specifically hardware and consulting services. A VRIO analysis might have looked something like the one in Table 1-3. Using the VRIO analysis might have led Insight to make the following resource-based strategic decisions:

- *Leverage* the distribution network by expanding offerings. Our operational excellence is a valuable strength—why not apply that to hardware?
- *Develop* additional and more exclusive licensing agreements, so we have an inimitable array of brand-name offerings.
- *Invest* in resources to provide technical support to our customers, building on the relationships we have to become a more comprehensive vendor.

While this is a hypothetical analysis, a company observer might note that the company did, in fact, move into hardware distribution and has many brand licensing agreements (company website) for both software and hardware. Insight also acquired Software Spectrum, Inc., purportedly to serve as a strong accelerator of Insight's evolution to a broad-based technology solutions advisor and provider, because of Software Spectrum's expertise in business-to-business IT services.[8] This was followed in 2008 by Insight's acquisition of Calence, LLC, a firm specializing in networking solutions, advanced communications, and managed services.[9] The technique of VRIO analysis is not terribly complicated or technical—you might actually view it as common sense. The key benefit of this technique comes from the dialogue and focus it encourages among key decision makers in the firm. It can

Table 1-3   A Resource-Based View (RBV) Example

Resource	Valuable?	Rare?	Inimitable?	Organized?
Licensing agreements	Yes	No	No	Yes
Distribution network	Yes	Yes	Yes	No
Partner relationships	Yes	Yes	No	Yes
Technical support	No	No	No	No
Customer relationship management	Yes	No	No	Yes

help build consensus about the need for and priority of resource acquisition, development, and leverage in the overall strategic plan of an organization.

Application and Reflection

1. Use the value matrix to evaluate one of your favorite service providers. Develop a table that follows the format of the value matrix.
2. Use the resource-based view to evaluate a company for which you have worked. Develop a VRIO analysis.

SUMMARY

Operations are a critical success factor for most organizations and can be a key element in their competitive advantage. Viewing the operational system as a transformation function that adds value to inputs to create outputs helps to identify non-value-adding activities, as well as ways to produce faster, better, and/or cheaper results.

A three-pronged view of strategy integrates the domains of operations management, sales/marketing, and finance/accounting to create a value proposition that is distinctive, understood, and feasible.

The resource-based view of the firm in general, and VRIO analysis in particular, can facilitate decisions to enhance or develop resources for further competitive advantage.

Review Questions

1. Operations transform inputs into outputs by _____.
   a. handling material
   b. creating a competitive advantage
   c. adding value
   d. manufacturing
2. Which of the following is *not* an elemental transformation function?
   a. Alter
   b. Manufacture
   c. Inspect
   d. Transport

3. Inputs are strictly tangible.
   a. True
   b. False
4. Waste is considered to be an output.
   a. True
   b. False
5. Which of the following is *not* one of the ways in which operations management contributes to a firm's competitive advantage?
   a. By creating a perceived need
   b. By adding value to a combination of inputs
   c. By delivering a better service
   d. By manufacturing products faster
6. A prudent business leader has a financial perspective of strategy that drives operational and marketing decisions.
   a. True
   b. False
7. A resource is rare if _____.
   a. it is valuable
   b. competitors do not have it
   c. it makes the firm competitive
   d. it is protected by patent
8. A resource may be considered inimitable if an underlying path dependency created it.
   a. True
   b. False

2

A PRACTICAL APPROACH TO OPERATIONS

The whole is more than the sum of the parts.
—ARISTOTLE

In Chapter 1, we examined an operational process as something that adds value to inputs to create outputs. One of the benefits of looking at organizations in this way is that it helps to identify sources of competitive advantage, as we saw with the value matrix and resource-based view techniques. While potentially useful, such results are only ideas on paper. To determine how we can manage the operation to achieve the desired results, we must extend our view of the transformation process a bit to consider the process as part of an overall system and then apply systems thinking to manage for the results we want to achieve.

After completing this chapter, you should be able to do the following:

- Explain how *systems thinking* impacts decision making
- Evaluate a business operation as a system

- Identify situations of *suboptimization*
- Apply a *business research* framework to identify opportunities for operational improvements

By understanding systems thinking, you will be able to apply a practical approach to a wide range of operational issues.

SYSTEMS THINKING

Simply put, a system is a dynamic, purposeful collection of components. Information and materials flow among these components. A system has boundaries; that which is outside the boundaries is considered the system's *environment*. Generally, the environment is considered to be outside the system's control; open systems are affected by their environment, whereas closed systems are not. *Feedback loops* provide information from one part of a system to another for purposes of adjusting the system's operation.

There are various types of systems, and they are characterized by their complexity. The number of components and subsystems, the presence of feedback loops, and the nature of the boundaries can all add to a system's complexity. Organizational systems tend to be quite complex, with multiple subsystems, numerous feedback loops, and permeable boundaries (meaning the organization interacts with its environment). In addition to current and potential rivals, customers, and suppliers,[1] environmental factors include political, economic, social, technological, environmental, and legal (*PESTEL*) factors.[2]

Origins of Systems Thinking

Systems thinking, as a formalized discipline, was a by-product of World War II.[3] We are surrounded by systems: ecosystems, social systems, transportation systems, and more. Each of us is a complex biological system with many subsystems, such as vascular, skeletal, and pulmonary. Understanding that a system's operation depends on the performance and interrelationships of its parts has been useful in a wide range of applications, including philosophy, engineering, and the sciences. Key aspects of systems thinking in management are the emphasis on *holism*, the focus on processes, the interdisciplinary perspective, and the use of feedback loops or mechanisms for system improvement.[4]

This sounds pretty abstract, but there are practical implications of systems thinking. An emphasis on holism suggests that it does not make sense to focus improvements in one area of an operation if it has a detrimental effect on another part of the system. A focus on processes highlights the interdependencies in the operational system. In the same way, considering sales perspectives as well as engineering considerations leads to a more robust and effective operation. Feedback—providing data and information about materials, processes, and results—is a hallmark of effective systems.

Arguably, the need for managers to apply systems thinking is increasing. The overall complexity of operational systems can be confounding. With the increasing pressures to make decisions more quickly, a holistic, process-oriented perspective is essential to avoid unintended consequences. Managing an operation with systems thinking can broaden a manager's perspective beyond a particular subsystem and provide new insights to improve its effectiveness. Using feedback mechanisms provides timely data for process improvement. As a result, the organization can avoid suboptimization, encourage data-based decision making, and improve operational robustness. This can sound daunting, but what it really means is that the manager can work smarter to achieve the desired results.

Systems Thinking in Operations

In Chapter 1, you were introduced to the idea of an operation as a transformation system, one that transforms inputs into outputs by adding value. A similar perspective describes an operation more broadly, transcending organizational boundaries with the concept of a *value chain*. The organizational system becomes even more complex, including suppliers, subcontractors, and even customers, when you examine the chain of activities by which value is added.

In the model developed by Michael Porter, the value chain of activities are categorized as either primary or secondary. Primary activities are directly involved in the transformation system and include inbound logistics, operations, outbound logistics, marketing and sales, and service. Secondary activities can also add value but are mostly conducted to enable the primary activities to be done. They include general administration, human resource management, technology management, and financial processes.[5]

Value chain analysis (VCA) is the epitome of systems thinking. The metaphor of a chain requires looking at the combination of activities as a whole, while recognizing the interdependencies among them. With advances in information systems and management practices, organizational boundaries are blurred, but the focus sharpens when value is added and waste is eliminated.

Suboptimization of Operational Systems

A lack of systems thinking leads to the issue of *suboptimization*, a problem that is rampant in many organizations. It often starts with an improvement in one department. This improvement might be optimal for that department, which is great, but the department is part of an operational system, and the impact of the improvement on other parts of the system has probably been overlooked. As a result, the performance of the overall system is less than it can be, or suboptimal.

This may be clearer with a few examples. Early in my career, I worked for IBM in sales and technical support. Unfortunately, I worked at one of the branches recognized for "administrative excellence." This location was terrific at submitting reports and forecasts on a timely basis, collecting outstanding accounts receivable, and managing expenses. However, the professional staff spent far more time on paperwork in the office than on selling and implementing new systems for customers in the field. In this case, the needs of one subsystem (administrative processes) dominated the needs of other components in the overall system. As a result, we optimized the average age of the office's accounts receivable, but we didn't maximize its profits.

I noted a different kind of suboptimization when I worked for the Quaker Oats Company, where I managed information systems in the late 1980s. Here, the organization tended to be optimized from a functional perspective. Marketing priorities routinely dominated decision making and funding, creating unbalanced performance in other areas. Sometimes the organization could not keep up with marketing initiatives, so expensive choices were made to satisfy demand. We will address ways in which to address capacity issues in a later chapter; for now, let's just say that short-term solutions tend to be costly. One colleague referred to this phenomenon as "air shipping concrete blocks."

This is not unlike the common scenario where budget and personnel cuts are made to meet short-term profitability targets for the stock market and investors. Optimizing for the short-term may not be in an organization's best interests for the long term. The financial results may look good, but the organization's ability to perform and compete is undermined.

Systems thinking is often referred to as "holistic," which means that the parts cannot be fully understood without examination of the whole. Psychologists use the term *gestalt* to emphasize the whole person in the context of his or her situation. *Holistic* is often used in medicine to suggest that physical symptoms should be treated with reference to psychological and social factors. Given a holistic view of an operational system, how do we decide how to "treat the patient"? How do we decide what changes to make in order to solve problems or otherwise make improvements? How do we avoid unintended consequences?

Our best thinking about management and operations stems from business research studies that have tested organizational theories, particularly in the wake of the Industrial Revolution. (That is not to suggest that management practices did not exist before then; surely the pyramids of Egypt are a testimony to very effective project management!) Whether you consider that we are now in the information, knowledge, or network age, you will find that a business research framework can still inform management practice.[6]

How can we separate the wheat from the chaff—that is, apply sound business practices and avoid the debris from the management "fad du jour"? I believe the most effective managers are those who (1) use systems thinking and (2) apply a business research framework to evaluate problems' solutions and improvement opportunities. This is the essence of our practical approach to operations management.

BUSINESS RESEARCH FRAMEWORK

The more I read (and the older I get), the more I become convinced that there are just a few really good ideas out there—each discipline just packages the concepts differently. So if you have studied the *scientific method* somewhere along the way, you'll find that business research is really the scientific method applied to questions in the context of businesses. The intent is to provide an objective, systematic, and logical basis for decision making.

Since we rarely have the controlled environment of a laboratory and a finite number of characteristics to study, business research tends to be "messier" than typical scientific research, meaning it is harder to replicate (something that works great in my business may be less effective in yours because of differences in your overall system or environment). Yet the process is remarkably the same:

1. Define the research question.
2. Develop *hypotheses* to test.
3. Collect the necessary data.
4. Analyze the results.
5. Take action, monitor, and repeat as needed.

Let's examine each step in more detail to see how the research framework is helpful for businesses.

Define the Research Question

The research question stems from a business need. The need may be precipitated by a breakdown in the operational process, an initiative in the strategic plan, a change in the operational system's environment, or ongoing continuous improvement efforts. Generally, you want to change things for the better. But how do you know what will make things better? That is the basis of the research question.

For example, let's say one of your suppliers goes out of business. This will cause an interruption in production unless you do something. That is a problem. What's the best thing to do? Well, it depends. On what? It depends on what is "best" for this operation. Do you want to minimize disruption? Minimize cost? Maximize flexibility? Your feasible solutions may range from switching the supply order to another provider, redesigning the product to eliminate the need for that supply, bringing the capability to supply that need in-house, or using this supplier issue as an opportunity to try offshore manufacturing. Make sure you are solving the right problem by asking the right question: what are the desired results?

Perhaps you are not solving a problem per se, but addressing a question that is precipitated by development or execution of your organization's strategic plan. Business research can be used to improve the performance of a business system, especially when the actual objectives are operationally related to the effectiveness and/or efficiency of operational business processes.[7] It is still important to consider the question of how to achieve a goal broadly and generate a wide array of options before settling on a specific research question. Remember, the holistic perspective is part of systems thinking, so you will want to consider various approaches in different functional areas so you can thoroughly consider the possibilities for achieving your desired results. The research question ("How can we best achieve the desired results?") can then be stated using specific performance measures.

Develop Hypotheses to Test

After formulating the question in terms of the desired results and considering the possible options, you might have an idea of what would work best. Before jumping headlong into action, however, you should test whether your idea is correct. Hypotheses are testable statements of theory. In this context, a hypothesis states the theory that *x* option will achieve *y* result. In our example of the defunct supplier, the hypothesis might be as follows:

> Modifying the product design to eliminate the need for the supplier (*x*) is the easiest way to minimize disruption (*y*); acquiring the materials needed from an offshore supplier (*x*) is the best way to minimize cost (*y*); or developing the capability to supply our needs in-house (*x*) is the optimal way to maximize flexibility (*y*).

Think of *x* as a variable representing what you can do, and *y* as a variable representing what you want. Table 2-1 has more precise terminology and typical hypotheses in an operational context. The hypothesis, then, is a testable statement of the relationship between *x* and *y*.

Table 2-1   Hypotheses in a General Business Research Framework

	x		*y*
Terminology	Action Stimuli Cause Independent variable	Relates to	Result Response Effect Dependent variable
Supplier example	Redesigning Offshore sourcing Developing in-house capability	Leads to	Minimal disruption Minimum cost Maximum flexibility
Other types of operational variables and relationships	Changes in • product design • process form • layout • location • material flow • job skills • technology • inventory control	Increases/decreases/ varies with	Results such as • productivity • quality • throughput • revenues • responsiveness • flexibility • customer satisfaction

Collect the Necessary Data

There are many ways to test a hypothesis, all of which entail collecting some form of data. The data might be as simple as anecdotal evidence of others' experiences, a compilation of expert opinion (from either primary sources or secondary sources such as published reports), a simulation of the proposed approach, or the results from a controlled trial.

It is important to remember that collecting data has a cost. Generally, you will find that the more rigorous the test, the more valid the data—and the more expensive the collection process. You should be practical in your approach and match the rigor to the risk of being wrong. (Caution: you might consider this to be common sense.)

In the case of the defunct supplier, let's assume that the desired result is to minimize disruption and that you think the best way to do this is by slightly modifying your product design to eliminate the need for that supplier's part. How should you test this? Consider the risk of being wrong. Risk is the product of the probability of being wrong and the cost of being wrong: $R = P \times C$, where R is the risk, P is the probability, and C is the cost.

In this case, the risk of being wrong is actually negligible; you may believe you can use a simpler, off-the-shelf sensor that has recently become available instead of the custom device you were purchasing. You can simply pull some of the assembled products and substitute the simpler sensor; if it works, you will know immediately. To consider the long-term risks of failure, you might take a random sample of products with the new sensor in them and run them in a stress test to see if they will fail any sooner or later than those with the old sensor.

Sometimes it really is that simple. In the consumer goods industry, research and development money is often invested in considering substitutable ingredients to avoid supplier disruptions, to extend shelf life, or to reduce the cost of goods sold. However, in a reactive situation such as our scenario, you must make sure you are thoroughly assessing the risk. It is extremely hard for an organization to overcome loss of life or a stain on its high-quality reputation. *Product recalls* are expensive in time, money, and brand equity.

Analyze the Results

This step may seem straightforward, but there are several pitfalls to avoid. First, realize that you may have three different outcomes: "Yes, this will achieve the desired results"; "No, we need to try something else"; or "It looks like we need more data." As you proceed to act on these outcomes, beware of the following potential pitfalls.

The precision of the insights from testing is limited by the data—and some people are never satisfied. You may need to press on despite the "paralysis of analysis" that can often overcome this step in business research. We all make decisions based on imperfect information, and occasionally the right answer *will* be to do more testing. But if you have followed the methodology thoroughly, then trust your results and your judgment.

Remember that numbers are not always fully numerical, so do not perform inappropriate calculations. This often happens when surveys are used for business research. For example, a company wants to measure its customers' satisfaction after implementing a new call center approach. If the survey data on gender are coded as 1 = female and 0 = male, then do not average them! In this case, the numbers are *nominal*, meaning they are just names or labels for convenience. While that may be common sense, a more insidious trap is averaging responses from a Likert scale, where the survey asks for the respondent to rate something from 1 to 5 or 1 to 10. Unless you can justify that the difference between 1 and 2 is the same difference as between 3 and 4 (which it probably is not, if you're asking for an opinion), then you should consider these numbers to be *ordinal*. That means the numerical value is really just a rank relative to the order of the other numbers. In this case, you could use the median (but not the arithmetic mean) to get an "average" response. The mean is an appropriate measure for interval (that is, $6 - 5 = 10 - 9$) or ratio (50:5 becomes 10:1 numbers).

Another caveat to remember is that correlation does not imply causation. Be careful when analyzing results that you do not overstate the relationship between your x and your y. For example, a not-for-profit enterprise wondered if its annual fund-raising auction might be more successful if the dress code were casual rather than formal. The first year the committee tried a relaxed dress code, donations increased. Was it because people were dressed differently? One argument in support of this interpretation is that people were more comfortable and spent more time at the event. But it might also be that the event attracted a different set of supporters who preferred to spend money to support the cause rather than to buy new clothes for the event. Or it is possible that neither of these interpretations is true, and some other factor, such as the weather, largely led to the increase in donations.

One other caution: avoid sampling on the *dependent variable*. That sounds technical, but it means that y is a variable that can have various values. This is often overlooked when you are studying successful companies to gain a sense of their best practices. It is important to look at comparable companies that have not been successful. Otherwise, you might conclude that the CEOs of all successful companies wear wristwatches; therefore, you should wear one too, so your company will be successful. It seems to be human nature to generalize about a few success cases without considering any failures. Nothing fuels career progression faster than learning from other people's mistakes.

Cause and effect are often separated in time and space.[8] Fixing a problem in the short term may create problems elsewhere in the system over the long term. Or as renowned systems thinker Peter Senge noted, "Today's problems come from yesterday's solutions."[9] It is important to consider how the operational system works over time. It is also crucial to look beyond the proximal cause of a problem or opportunity to identify the root cause.

There is an old adage: "Give a man a fish, he eats for a day; teach a man to fish, he eats for life." Rather than overwhelm you with the specific (and typically perishable and oversimplified) techniques that proliferate in operations management textbooks, my intent is to ground your understanding of operations management in systems thinking and a research framework. In that way, as opportunities present themselves, you will be prepared to evaluate them in the context of your own operation and its operating environment.

Take Action, Monitor, and Repeat as Needed

Whenever possible, it is advisable to implement a solution on a limited scale to enable you to better gauge the full impact of your decision. This might be accomplished by piloting the solution or improvement in a limited area of the operation, such as with one product line, one retail location, or one supplier. Depending on the nature of the change, a pilot test may identify procedural issues, training needs, capacity challenges, and other glitches. It may also help you develop a "proof of concept," providing credible evidence of feasibility to ease the implementation elsewhere in the operation.

Even if a gradual implementation is not feasible, it is essential that the change be monitored to assess its impact. Was the desired result achieved? Did it create unintended consequences? The results of monitoring should be communicated to all affected parties. If the desired results have not been achieved, then the business research process should be restarted to pursue other options.

TECHNIQUE: ENVIRONMENTAL ANALYSIS

In systems theory, the system's environment is composed of those factors outside its control that have an impact on its operation. In businesses, a common technique for identifying environmental forces is to use the PESTEL analysis I mentioned earlier, which examines political, economic, social, technological, environmental (in the traditional sense), and legal factors.[10] For example, if your company manufactures educational toys, your PESTEL analysis might consider the following environmental factors:

- **Political:** An oil embargo from Venezuela could increase the cost of fuel and petroleum-based polymers, thus reducing your products' contribution margins.
- **Economic:** Rising unemployment may dampen demand for your product.
- **Social:** An increasing number of single-parent households may increase demand for your toys in day care and after-school care facilities.
- **Technological:** The availability of inexpensive programmable chips might provide an opportunity to enhance the interactivity of the toys.
- **Environmental:** An increasing number of options for alternative energy sources may require modifying the production flow.
- **Legal:** A change in trade legislation may affect your ability to produce or sell your products abroad.

By understanding your operating environment, you are in a better position to anticipate changes and avoid suboptimal decisions.

Another popular approach for environmental analysis is Michael Porter's *Five Forces model*, which evaluates the impact of customers, suppliers, competitors, substitutes, and the government on a company's competitive advantage.[10] At the level of an operational system, it is often decisions driven by other areas of the business that have an impact on the operation's effectiveness. For example, marketing and brand development may want to add or change existing products. Purchasing agents may order from different suppliers. Human resource management may negotiate a new set of terms and conditions with the workers' union. As an operations manager, you must be alert to the environmental factors that are most likely to have an impact on your operation's effectiveness.

Application and Reflection

1. In your organization, what feedback loops are used for management decision making and control? Be specific.
2. Consider a scenario in which a doctor's office is receiving complaints from patients about waiting time. Develop several hypotheses of possible causes, following the format in Table 2-1, earlier in this chapter.
3. In what situations have you experienced suboptimal decisions? What was being optimized, and what was the detrimental effect?

SUMMARY

Applying systems thinking can broaden a manager's perspective beyond a particular subsystem and provide new insights to improve its effectiveness. As a result, an organization can avoid suboptimization, encourage data-based decision-making, and improve operational robustness.

Like any system, a business operation is a dynamic, purposeful collection of components, and material and information flow among these components.

Organizational systems tend to be complex, with multiple subsystems, numerous feedback loops, and permeable boundaries with the environment (factors outside the system's control). Understanding key factors in an operation's environment puts the manager in a better position to anticipate changes and avoid suboptimal decisions.

By applying the scientific method to organizational issues and managerial questions, business research can provide an objective, systematic, and logical basis for decision making. Pitfalls to avoid in business research include overstating the precision of the research, applying quantitative analysis inappropriately, assuming causation from a correlation, sampling on the dependent variable, and ignoring the dynamics of the operational system over time.

Review Questions

1. Which of the following is *not* typically part of a system?
   a. Feedback loops
   b. Boundaries

   c. Components
   d. Environment
   e. All of the above

2. A system's environment is defined by the weather conditions it faces.
   a. True
   b. False

3. Which of the following is *not* an environmental factor for operational systems?
   a. Politics
   b. Customers
   c. Corporate culture
   d. Suppliers
   e. All of the above

4. Why do we use systems thinking in operations management?
   a. Human bodies are complex biological systems.
   b. An operation's performance depends on the performance and interrelationship of its parts.
   c. It has been used since World War I.
   d. Engineers find it useful.

5. Effective systems do not need feedback loops.
   a. True
   b. False

6. Which of the following describes suboptimization?
   a. Optimizing one aspect of an operation to the detriment of the operation as a whole
   b. Achieving less-than-optimal results with a decision
   c. Being useful in the resolution of subsystem problems
   d. Applying a holistic technique for system improvement
   e. All of the above

7. A business research framework can be used instead of systems thinking for effective operations management.
   a. True
   b. False

8. Which of the following is *not* part of a business research process?
   a. Defining the problem
   b. Collecting necessary data
   c. Analyzing the environment
   d. Taking action
   e. All of the above are part of a business research process.

9. "Numbers are not always fully numerical" means that
   a. some arithmetic functions may not apply to a specific data set.
   b. data collection can be suboptimal.
   c. correlation does not imply causation.
   d. you need to use at least two decimal places to be fully numerical.
   e. some people will not understand presentations of numerical data.

10. PESTEL analysis examines the competitive environment and the threat of substitutes.
    a. True
    b. False

3

DESIRED RESULTS

Not everything that can be counted counts, and not
everything that counts can be counted.
—ALBERT EINSTEIN

A s I write this chapter, I cannot help but recall two important
life lessons from my early career. The first came from my
very first professor—in the first class meeting—in my M.B.A.
program. He walked into the lecture hall, put his materials
down on the front desk, and said without any introduction,
"Accountants measure irrelevancies with precision." This was strongly rein-
forced years later, when Goldratt and Cox first published the book *The Goal*
and lambasted measurement systems that focused on individual efficiencies,
machine utilizations, balancing capacities, and other counterproductive measures. Just because you *can* measure something, it does not mean that it is
the right thing to measure. However, I do believe strongly that you cannot
manage what you cannot measure.

The other key lesson came from someone I reported to in the corporate world. At one point, when I was complaining about a pointless task a
customer had asked for, he said kindly, "Whenever anyone asks you to jump,

you say, 'How high?' when what you should really be asking is 'Why?'" This insight has had wide-reaching implications for me, most particularly the need for clarity about desired results, whether for a client, a customer, a colleague, or myself. Because the bottom line is that unless you know what the bottom line is, you are unlikely to achieve the desired results. The corollary to this principle is that to know that you have achieved the desired results, you need measurements.

After completing this chapter, you should be able to do the following:

- Distinguish between desired results, *constructs*, and *indicators* of success
- Define *productivity* in the context of any organization
- Apply basic principles of *measurement*
- Relate operational decision making to organizational *performance*
- Develop a multidimensional measurement system

As we have seen so far, operational systems can be very complex and therefore have innumerable possibilities for measurement. If a system produces services, we have additional measurement challenges stemming from the intangible and experiential nature of services. In this chapter, we extend our conceptual foundation to include measurement theory, which leads us to our general model of operational decision making.

MEASUREMENT THEORY

Perhaps the hardest concept in measurement theory is the idea that what you measure (the indicator) is not the thing you measure (the construct). For example, imagine that it is a rainy Saturday afternoon and you find yourself shopping for furniture—in particular, a table. At home, you have a favorite chair to read in, but you need somewhere to place a lamp and a coaster. You find a table you really like, but you want to measure it before you bring it home. Think for a moment: how might you measure a table (the construct)? You could certainly measure height, width, length, weight, durability, stability, price, and more. You might also measure in terms of numerical count: number of nicks, number of coasters or picture frames it could comfortably accommodate, and so on. Each of these possible measures is an indicator of the table but is not the table itself. Note also that the table is not really the desired result; it is a way to satisfy your need for a lamp and a place to hold a drink while you are reading.

When developing a measurement system, it is important to first define the desired results and then to define the appropriate constructs and their relation to the desired results. The challenge then becomes what indicators can and should be measured to provide valid insight into performance. As an illustration, consider a food service distributor whose owner wants to increase the company's profitability (desired result). She believes that if the company can increase its productivity (construct), profitability will improve. The underlying hypothesis is that the distributor can keep satisfied customers while increasing output and/or decreasing input. The question then becomes what measures she should use to test this hypothesis?

In civil engineering and land surveying, they use a technique called *triangulation*, which is based on Euclidean geometry. In management, we use that term as a metaphor to emphasize the use of multiple (but not necessarily three) sources and/or methodologies for measurement. This increases the integrity of the evaluation, which means you are getting a truer assessment of the construct. Triangulation is especially important when evaluating services operations due to the difficulty of getting objective measures of intangible and experiential constructs.

Using only one measure is likely to create unintended consequences. As IBM's former chairman and chief executive officer, Louis Gerstner, Jr., noted, "People do what you *inspect*, not what you *expect*."[1]

For example, the food service distributor could institute a measure of number of deliveries per driver. This might encourage the drivers to hurry, but it might also lead to accidents or other costly mistakes. A construct like productivity has to be measured carefully.[2] The idea is to produce the desired result (output) with a minimum of effort (input). You want to measure both input and output, and you use multiple measures for both.

In addition to using triangulation to improve the validity of your measures, consider using the dimension of time to gain insight into the operation's performance. How can a temporal series of data inform your decision making? You might detect cycles, trends, or anomalies by examining your results over time.

This is probably common sense to most of us, especially if we are in the habit of weighing ourselves in the morning. If we find that we tend to weigh more on Mondays than on Fridays, then we might be having too much fun on the weekends and can think about what we should do to avoid such fluctuations. If I step on the scale and find that I have lost several pounds overnight, I wait to make sure that the measure is consistent over the next several days before I start celebrating. If it is, I have a trend; if it is not, then it was an anomaly.

My last piece of advice about measurement systems is to audit them periodically. Are the data being gathered on a consistent basis? Are the measures being taken accurately? Are they easy to understand and report? Are they being used to inform decision making? Do the costs of measurement outweigh the benefits of data collection? Are you achieving your desired results and fulfilling your mission?

To recap, good measurement systems have the following characteristics:

- They relate the desired results to the construct being measured.
- They use valid indicators, triangulation, and time series to measure the construct.
- They are audited periodically.[3]

As we will see, operational measures can inform a wide range of decisions.

OPERATIONAL DECISION MAKING

There are two types of decisions to be made: operational and otherwise. Operational decisions affect all aspects of an organization. It may help to think of the organization's mission statement as defining what it does to add value and for whom; it follows that operational decisions impact how the organization fulfills its mission.

The typical operations textbook illustrates this breadth of decision making with an inevitable survey of topics and techniques. Decision domains of product and service design, process selection, project management, technological applications, facility layout, job design, process analysis, capacity management, forecasting, inventory control, sequencing, scheduling, resource acquisition and allocation, location selection, quality assurance, continuous improvement, and management control are all within the purview of operations management. Operations strategy, as we have already seen, affects an organization's competitive advantage.

Emerging Trends in Measuring Operations

Lean production, supply chain management, and *Six Sigma* are specific operational strategies that cross over several decision domains and emphasize the need for a systems view of the organization. These topics will be addressed in more detail in later chapters. Here, the point is that such strategies are highly data-driven, using closely monitored metrics that cross organizational boundaries. Complexity, to some extent, drives the need for measurement to ensure that the desired results are achieved.

Complexity also drives the need for measurement to ensure that there are no undesirable effects. Life cycle assessment (*LCA*) is an emerging practice that examines the ecological effects of the production, consumption, and disposal of products. It entails documenting the minutiae of manufacturing—what materials and how much energy are used, what kinds of pollution are generated and toxins exuded, and in what amounts—for each basic unit in a very long chain.[4]

In the aluminum industry, LCA extends past bauxite mining, its refinement to aluminum oxide, and production of aluminum to how it is used in fabrication. This includes environmental and economic effects of the fabrication and the use of the end result (such as the resulting reduction of car emissions). LCA also encompasses recycling and reuse of a material in new products.[5]

Fundamental Measures for Operations

As we consider the breadth of decisions to be made in an operational system, it may help to realize that desired results can be categorized more simply. Think of the decision in terms of "Now, and in the future, will this action help us to deliver value in any of the following ways?"

- Faster (with lower response time or greater throughput)
- Better (with higher quality or greater customer satisfaction)
- Cheaper (with higher productivity or lower operating costs)
- Differently (with greater flexibility or more innovation)

Each of these four areas of desired results can have a bottom-line impact on the organization.

Traditionally, though, managers have relied on financial measures and argued over cost allocations and budget variances to manage their operations. While financial measures are necessary, they are not sufficient to manage an operational system. Common sense, right? When Kaplan and Norton first introduced the idea of a *balanced scorecard* in their article about broader-based measurement in the *Harvard Business Review*, it was an idea whose time had finally come.[6]

TECHNIQUE: THE BALANCED SCORECARD

Kaplan and Norton reported on an approach they had used to balance financial measures with nonfinancial measures for management and control. These measures should be aligned with the strategic plan of the organization. The balance in the scorecard of measures is between internal and external perspectives, as well as between short- and long-term perspectives. The scorecard provides an at-a-glance look at key measures, generally in the following areas:

- Financial
- Customers
- Business processes
- Learning and growth

These categories may be adapted to an industry context, but the idea of balance should persist. For example, the category of customers for a consumer goods producer might be extended to include consumers, since it must satisfy both the retailers and the end users who purchase the goods. Measurements might include the volume of returned or defective goods, which represent lost sales to the manufacturer. In retail, scanner data provide a wealth of opportunity for gauging success, such as brand X purchases per customer or product A combined in a purchase with a competitor's version of product B.

Employee satisfaction and turnover rates are commonly used to gauge learning and growth. In a high-tech industry, a manufacturer may want to represent measures for learning and growth as metrics for innovation to stress the importance of innovation in that industry. It might be appropriate to track the number of active patents, the number of new patents in a month, the number of research projects in the final testing phase, and so on. Since the firm wants to be innovative, it must identify critical success factors for innovation and measure them.

For operations management, metrics in the areas of operational excellence, customer intimacy, product leadership, and financial performance may be more relevent.[7] Other considerations such as customer aggravation, employee satisfaction, and employee health and safety should not be overlooked either.[8] As an operations manager, you should strive to understand your business's drivers.

Academically, business drivers are independent variables (see Chapter 2) that are typically abstract constructs. The key is to link performance measures (indicators) to key success factors (constructs) as identified in the organization's strategic plan (desired results). As a rule of thumb, it may help to note that measurements can be expressed as numerical values per unit or as a percentage.

A variety of formats can be used to present a scorecard.[9] When computer-based, the scorecard is often condensed to a "dashboard" format, providing a graphical, at-a-glance view and drill-down capability (to examine the detail behind the summary measures). Colors may be used to highlight outliers, or measures that are below specified targets. For example, the use of yellow might convey a warning that a metric is slipping below expectations, and red might indicate an unacceptable situation. The operations manager can use the scorecard to prioritize issues and dig more deeply into the data.

In my experience, one other perspective should be balanced in the organization's scorecard. To really promote communications and linkage at departmental levels, there should be a balance between organizational measures and department or unit measures. For example, I worked with a consulting company that was trying to achieve strategic changes in its organization. It was clear that the emphasis on individuals' "billability"—the amount of working hours that were charged to clients—was impeding the implementation of growth initiatives in general and a business team concept in particular.

In the scorecard that I prepared, measures were linked back to specific goals in the company's strategic plan. Measures had to be credible to the consultants, which meant that (1) it was clear how each metric related to a strategic goal; (2) objective data were used; and (3) the metrics were based on performance the consultants could influence, that is, they were actionable process metrics and not measures of end results. As scorecard pioneer Art Schneiderman explained:

> [D]ieters often tend to focus on their body weight (a results metric) rather than its independent [process] measures: exercise along with calorie, protein, fat, and carbohydrate consumption. Nutritionists now believe that successful diets involve lifestyle (aka process) changes that act on these independent measures. Get them right and over time you will achieve and sustain your weight goal.[10]

As mentioned in Chapter 2, introducing a change (like a scorecard) is best done on a small scale to make sure that appropriate measures have been identified. This is especially important when incentive and compensation systems are tied to scorecard results. It is advisable to run the scorecard in a pilot test to determine whether you are getting the desired results and whether the compensation system reflects the performance appropriately.

It is not always easy to develop a complete set of appropriate metrics at the onset; the scorecard may evolve over time. For example, keeping track of how engaged and satisfied your employees are may be crucial, especially in a services organization where they are, in essence, your operational resources. Another thing to consider is that measuring customer aggravation may be more reliable and meaningful than measuring customer satisfaction.[11] You are more likely to hear from dissatisfied customers than from satisfied ones.

You should also be cautious about relying too heavily on measures that tell you what happened (like looking through the rear-view mirror), of performance and try to use metrics that can provide leading, or predictive, indicators of success.[12] For example, a grocery chain might determine that its customers with loyalty cards spend more per visit than other customers do. Management might then want to track the issuance of new loyalty cards as a leading indicator.

Let's close with a continuation of our food service distributor example, in which the owner wants to increase profitability (desired result). At a corporate and divisional level, she is using contribution margin as the indicator of productivity. Within each division, the sales executive focuses on overall sales targets and cost of goods sold as a percentage of overall sales. In one division in particular, the vice president of sales knows that it is more expensive to sell to a new customer than to an existing one, so he launches an initiative to encourage salespeople to spend more time understanding their current customers' requirements so they can maximize their account potential. The salespeople are given specific targets to reduce their customer churn rate and increase their sales per customer.

Measurement is foundational to operations management. Metrics inform decision making and demonstrate the impact of decisions on organizational performance. A measurement system, if used appropriately, can be a powerful tool to guide and motivate employees to achieve targeted performance improvements and, ultimately, desired results.

Application and Reflection

1. Develop internal performance measures for a hotel, long-term performance measures for a government contractor, customer perspective measures for a spa, and learning and growth perspective measures for a public accounting firm.

2. An e-tailer wants to increase its repeat business (desired result). To accomplish this, management wants to improve customer satisfaction (construct). What are appropriate indicators for customer satisfaction? How would data for those indicators be gathered? What are the pros and cons for using each of these measures?

SUMMARY

Measurements are evaluations of indicators of constructs, meaning what you measure is not the thing you measure. Measurement of services is especially challenging due to the often intangible and experiential nature of the operation. It is important to use a variety of measures to improve their validity.

Operational decisions can have a bottom-line impact on a corporation by improving ways to deliver value faster, better, cheaper, and differently. In particular, productivity is basically the amount of desired output resulting from a given level of input. It is important to measure both parts of the ratio of output to input.

You cannot manage what you cannot measure. You need to balance short- and long-term measures, internal and external perspectives, and organizational levels to evaluate your progress toward your desired results. You should also audit your measurement system periodically.

Review Questions

1. "You cannot manage what you cannot measure" means _____.
   a. only tangible goods can be measured
   b. it is important to measure with precision
   c. measurement provides clarity on the desired results
   d. you have to measure up as a manager
   e. None of the above

2. Indicators are measures of constructs.
   a. True
   b. False

3. Constructs represent the desired results.
   a. True
   b. False

4. It is best to use a single measure to keep the system simple.
   a. True
   b. False

5. Tracking a measurement over time is useful to _____.
   a. detect cycles
   b. identify anomalies
   c. collect temporal data
   d. a and b
   e. All of the above

6. Measurement systems should be audited to determine _____.
   a. if they are informing decision making
   b. if the cost of data collection is merited
   c. if measurements are being taking accurately
   d. b and c
   e. All of the above

7. Productivity is a measure of input need per measure of output.
   a. True
   b. False

8. Life cycle assessment (LCA) is a measure of _____.
   a. the total cost of ownership
   b. the ecological impact of products
   c. aluminum recycling
   d. a company's carbon footprint
   e. None of the above

9. Which of the following should be balanced in a balanced scorecard?
    a. Short- and long-term measures
    b. Internal and external perspectives
    c. Individual and group measures
    d. a and b
    e. All of the above
10. A balanced scorecard must contain financial, customer, business process, and learning and growth measures.
    a. True
    b. False

4

ORGANIZATIONAL PERFORMANCE

Only the mediocre are always at their best.
—JEAN GIRAUDOUX

The operational decision that drives all other operational decisions is "What product/service will we offer?" The answer drives *organizational performance*. Decisions about product or service development determine what inputs are required; influence decisions about capacity, layout, and location; and influence sales, marketing, and distribution efforts. The entire *value chain* is affected.

After completing this chapter, you should be able to do the following:

- Describe the stages of product and service design and development
- Identify *trade-offs* in design factors
- Distinguish between different types of *production processes*
- Explain the *service matrix*
- Perform a simple *quality function deployment* (*QFD*)

PRODUCT AND SERVICE DESIGN AND DEVELOPMENT

The new product/service development (*NPD/NSD*, or known separately as *NPD* or *NSD*) process typically begins in one of two ways: *technology push* or *market pull*. Technology push occurs as a result of innovation in the value chain. Perhaps a new form of an input is available, or the limitations of a transformation process have changed. The market is unaware of the new possibilities, and demand must be created by "pushing" the new product into the marketplace.

An example that comes to mind is new software releases, particularly for desktop computing. I have used Quicken to track finances and pay bills for more than 10 years. It seems like a new version with "new and improved" features is released every year. Yet I have never perceived a need for any of these new features. I may use a few of them once I have upgraded, but the impetus for the changes was technology push.

Market pull arises when customers' requirements drive innovation. For example, I always wanted my bank statements and credit cards to interface with Quicken directly so that I wouldn't have to enter every transaction manually. Gradually, the banks have responded to this market pull and now offer this service. Similarly, online bill payment is becoming more widely available. The technological capability has existed for years, but until the market demand was evident, institutions did not want to invest in the required infrastructure.

The technology push/market pull dichotomy is a broad characterization of NPD/NSD. To get to the point of having an actual new product or service, an idea will typically go through many stages of development and approval. As Nobel Laureate Linus Pauling is credited with saying, "If you want to have good ideas, you must have many ideas."

You can tell a lot about an organization by the way it performs in this area. Who is involved? Is there a formalized process? How are ideas funded? How are old products and services retired? (By the way, these are good questions to ask on an interview!)

Like any organizational process, the more stable (but not rigidly inflexible) the NPD/NSD process, the better results you can expect. Borrowing a term from nautical science, Abrahamson suggests that "dynamic stability" should be the goal of an organization.[1] The idea is that continual but relatively small change efforts enable companies to innovate. It is part of the corporate culture to expect—but also to pace—changes in a dynamically stable environment.

Typically, the process starts with what I refer to as an "organizational itch." Someone has perceived a need or an opportunity. This may come from the executive ranks, the bench scientists, or the field representatives. If the itch becomes an idea that seems promising, fits within the organization's mission, and does not detract from existing priorities, a limited amount of resources (time and money) will be allocated to explore it further.

Such exploration is considered a preliminary stage of feasibility analysis. This may be performed as a market research study (pull) or as prototype development (push). Once the idea is determined to be feasible, the next question is whether it is viable, that is, can the firm offer the product or service profitably? Will the market and margins be sufficient to recover development costs? Building a business case for the offering engages other parts of the organization—such as manufacturing engineering, sales and marketing, inventory management, warranty service, and distribution—for more precise cost estimates and risk analyses. With a promising business case, the next stage in the process is a pilot or test phase under limited production and delivery. Using lessons learned from this phase, adjustments are made before the product or service is fully rolled out. Even though this is presented as a rational, sequential process, it can be nonlinear and recursive. It is like any other organizational process, with inputs/outputs, feedback loops, and environmental factors.

The metaphor of a funnel can be helpful to understand this process, especially in highly innovative companies, such as in the pharmaceutical industry. Many ideas enter the funnel's opening. At each stage, more information is needed as more investment is made; progressively fewer product concepts pass through the funnel until one drug is approved for commercialization.

With larger organizations, it is important to look at NPD/NSD in the context of a "portfolio" of offerings. The portfolio should be diversified in terms of both product life cycle and resource allocation,[2] prompting certain questions. As the firm introduces its new platform product (one that is completely different from earlier offerings), are there mature products that should be retired? If the firm is doing a major upgrade to one product line, does it make sense to tackle a minor product upgrade elsewhere in the organization? The timing of these decisions must be examined collectively.

This life cycle perspective offers insight into the timing, or staging, of decisions. Basically, over the course of time, a product experiences different rates of growth, as depicted by Figure 4-1. Once past the introduction stage, prices are high and investment in technology is typically low and general

Figure 4-1   The Product Life Cycle

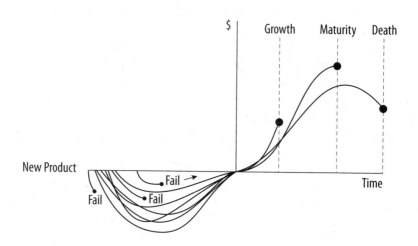

purpose. As the product grows to maturity and faces increasing competition, efficiency becomes more of a business driver. Prices may be lowered, and firms may invest in more specialized automation technology.

At this point, before the product begins to decline, it is essential to have "the next thing" ready. Are you going to extend the product's life cycle by upgrading it or offering it in new markets? Are you going to replace it? Or are you going to milk it dry? Once the product begins its decline toward death, it is very difficult to change that momentum.[3]

Trends in NPD/NSD

Not only are companies scrambling to develop the right products and services, they are racing to get it done ASAP. Time-based competitive pressures are increasing; IBM coined the phrase "on-demand economy" in recognition of this trend. One key to organizational performance, then, is the ability to streamline and compress NPD/NSD schedules.

In the manufacturing arena, the use of product development teams—including personnel from marketing, engineering, manufacturing, purchasing, and postsales support—is now common practice. You wouldn't think this was such a novel idea, but before we had product development teams, marketing came up with an idea and got engineering to work it through the research and development (R&D) process; once it was approved by upper management, it became the purview of the manufacturing folks to figure out how to actually produce it.

Now, with both R&D and manufacturing engineers on the development team, team members can perform *concurrent engineering* and ensure a *robust* design. Concurrence allows them to discuss implementation considerations and design for the manufacturability of the product, making it easier to transition into production. In my experience, R&D engineers think in terms of what is possible; manufacturing engineers think about what is practical. Technology can also facilitate this planning with computer-aided design (CAD) and manufacturing (CAM). Using three-dimensional models on a computer enables engineers to try alternatives, check clearances and stress points, and in some cases, translate the design into programs to control the manufacturing process. Trial and error on a computer is much less expensive than on the manufacturing floor.

When all affected departments work together, it tends to lead to a more robust design, or an offering that can be produced consistently despite the variability of environmental conditions, such as humidity and vibration. Purchasing agents can often contribute to this discussion, having a different perspective of the available materials needed to ensure robustness. They can also advocate for simplifying the number of direct materials; for example, "Do we really need a $^5/_{16}$-inch screw, or will the $^1/_4$-inch screws we keep in stock suffice?"

The product development team leader is not only responsible for the coordination of roles, responsibilities, and timelines, but should also fulfill the role of "enforcer" by consistently performing value analysis. This entails asking questions like, "Why are we doing this?" "Where is the value added?" and "Is this really necessary?" to ensure that design elements, process steps, and team effort are focused on what adds value for the customer.

Ultimately, streamlined NPD/NSD catches errors and design flaws earlier in the process. Think about building a house. Isn't it a lot less expensive to move a doorway on the blueprint than once the house has been framed— much less drywalled or bricked? The sooner, the better.

Another interesting trend in NPD/NSD is what General Electric (GE) has termed "*reverse innovation.*" A key part of the company's strategy is now anchored in developing countries. GE's management believes that the traditional process of developing products at home and then adapting them for other markets around the world will be inadequate as growth slows in rich nations. Instead, they have begun the development of products in countries like China and India. Once products have proven themselves in these emerging markets, they are then positioned for global distribution. For GE, this represents a dramatically different business model that is based on high volumes of low-priced products.[4] Note that the impetus is still market pull; the focus is just on a different market.

Reverse innovation might also be construed as *"disruptive innovation,"* by which the firm disrupts itself. This type of innovation occurs when a new product, at a lower price and level of performance than a mature product, overtakes the mature product's market. For example, consider cell phones. When they were first introduced, they were clunky and unreliable. The sound quality was far inferior to landline-based telephony. Over the years, though, cell phone technology has improved, the disrupted telephony life cycle has restarted, and wireless adoptions exceed wired installations.

Christiansen suggests that this is a common phenomenon caused by the "innovators' dilemma."[5] Successful companies lose to upstart competition because the entrenched firms make only marginal improvements to satisfy existing customers. The idea of producing something of lesser quality and performance seems paradoxical, hence the dilemma.

Consider the case of Xerox in the 1980s. Xerox was making increasingly fast and complicated printers and copiers; some of its models required special operating environments, and most were extremely large. Enter Ricoh, a Japanese company offering small, inexpensive copiers that were much slower and had limited functionality. What they did offer, as opposed to Xerox, was convenience. These small "convenience copiers" could be located in regular office space, providing quick and easy access for casual use. The Ricoh models represented a disruptive innovation, which Xerox had overlooked, and created a new life cycle for xerography.

Trade-Offs in Design Factors

A common pitfall in NPD/NSD is inherent in the trade-offs that must be made. The way a product or service is designed has far-reaching implications for an organization's operational system and overall effectiveness.

The introduction of field-replaceable units (FRUs) at IBM is an interesting case in point. As mainframe computers became increasingly vital to business operations, outages became extremely expensive for IBM's customers. So customers were willing to pay more for hardware maintenance if it came with availability guarantees where they were assured of the "up" time of the computer. How could IBM provide that assurance? The mainframes were extremely reliable but not infallible. Field engineers could be dispatched quickly in the case of an outage, but problem determination could be time-consuming. So IBM largely took the problem determination out of the outage timeline. Instead of having to swap out individual components to determine the point of failure, field engineers could quickly narrow down which subsystem was the problem and then just swap in a new FRU (a collection of components) for that subsystem. The old FRU could be diagnosed and repaired offline and perhaps redeployed as a replacement FRU in the future. The decision to move to FRUs had an impact on how the mainframes were designed, how spare parts inventories were maintained, how service contracts were negotiated with customers, and how the field engineers were trained. The FRUs were more expensive than individual spare parts, but that was offset by the revenue opportunities of better service agreements and the time and training cost of the field engineers.

For a service industry example, consider a restaurant chain owner who wants to expand her offerings to include more grilled items in addition to her Southern-fried specialties. She is responding to customer requests and hopes to appeal to new customers who eschew fried foods, thereby increasing restaurant sales. Here are some trade-offs she may need to consider:

- Can the existing food service supplier provide the fresh items needed to have a quality grilled entrée, or do we have to find a new supplier?
- Is there enough refrigerator space to keep the ingredients fresh, enough grill space to accommodate anticipated demand, and so on, or do we have to eliminate some existing menu items?
- Do any changes to the layout, such as for ventilation needs, need to be implemented first? Will that have an impact on other work flows?
- Is the staff in the kitchen and dining room prepared, so that timing orders and serving them hot are not an issue, or should we hire more experienced staff (or invest in training for existing staff)?
- How much inventory should be kept at each location? We may lose customers if we don't have enough, but we do not want to have so much that it spoils before it is sold.

This is the essence of any decision making—balancing between trade-offs. Which is more beneficial in the product design of a briefcase, to be lightweight or sturdy? To ramp up capacity, should our company move to a second shift and hire more workers, or should it ask already trained employees to work overtime? Should we automate to be more efficient, or should we sustain our existing flexibility? Should we maintain a finished goods inventory or allow orders to be backlogged? If there aren't any trade-offs, then there's not much of a decision to make.

Sometimes the trade-offs are between the potential benefits and the risks inherent in realizing them. For example, you might pick exactly the right component for the product you are launching, but the supplier is a brand-new start-up company. Are you willing to take the risk that supply might be interrupted or unreliable? Or if you buy a lower-grade direct material to save a little money, will that have a perceptible impact on your overall production quality?

One set of trade-offs that is often ill-considered is the total cost of ownership (TCO), which explicitly considers short- and long-term costs of a product. For example, a manufacturer may use less expensive materials to save on direct costs but encounter high warranty and repair expenses. Ferrin and Plank identified 13 categories of TCO cost drivers: operations cost, quality, logistics, technological advantage, supplier reliability and capability, maintenance, inventory cost, transaction cost, life cycle, initial price, customer related, opportunity cost, and miscellaneous costs.[6] Any two of these drivers represent a potential trade-off decision.

This is related to the idea of reliability, which is one key way to "design and manufacture for quality." Product or service reliability is a quantitative measure but represents how well a component, service, or system is able to perform as intended under expected conditions. It affects buyers' assessment of value and the product's (and company's) image, and of course, it has legal implications in terms of liability. Reliability is usually stated as a probability and defined in terms of failure: $R = 1 - P(F)$, where R = reliability; P = probability and F = failure, meaning a part of a product or system does not perform as intended (whether it does not operate at all, gives substandard performance, or has unintended consequences). The probability may be in terms of function during any given trial or over a certain length of time. So it is important to be specific about the prescribed operating conditions for a product.

Of course, some organizations, afraid of litigation, take this warning too far. The Foundation for Fair Civil Justice (http://legalreforminthenews .com) publishes annual awards for "wacky warnings." Here is one from its website:

> The contest reveals how lawsuits and the fear of lawsuits have driven companies to spend millions on common-sense warnings. The 2009 winner is a submission from Steve Shiflett of Hampton, Georgia. The label is attached to a portable toilet seat for

outdoorsmen called "The Off-Road Commode" because it is designed to attach to a vehicle's trailer hitch. The warning label reads "Not for use on moving vehicles."

On a more serious note, reliability can be improved with decisions such as improving individual components (through design and purchasing) or providing redundancy with backup components.

After developing the product or service, the process of delivery is another decision. Here again there are trade-offs to be made. How much do you want to invest up front versus over the long run? How many whatchamacallits do you have to make to break even on an initial investment in technology?

There's a general trade-off in technological investments: flexibility versus efficiency. This can be seen in the product-process matrix in Figure 4-2. Think about the difference in the way Rolls-Royce produces a hand-

Figure 4-2   The Product-Process Matrix

Process Structure Process Life Cycle Stage ↓	Process Structure Process Life Cycle Stage →	Low Volume Unique (One of a Kind)	Low Volume Multiple Products	Higher Volume Standardized Product	Very High Volume Commodity Product
	(Project)				
Jumbled Flow (Job Shop)		Job Shop			
Disconnected Line Flow (Batch)			Batch		
Connected Line Flow (Assembly Line)				Assembly Line	
Continuous Flow (Continuous)					Continuous

built automobile versus the way a mass production line turns out Audi A4s (or better yet, watch "Rolls Royce Phantom Assembly" and "Audi A4 on the Production Line" at youtube.com). The level of automation is greater for the product made in higher volume, leading to higher efficiencies. Due to the investment in technology and the programming required for the robotic assembly, it is more difficult to make modifications to the Audi.

Understanding the appropriate process form is a key aspect of organizational performance. In a services illustration, a hospital is often considered as having a job shop process. Patients will have a "jumbled flow" (that is, experience a different sequence of events) based on their health care concerns. Management science, which has traditionally focused on manufacturing job shops, can provide some insight into hospital scheduling, department locations, and equipment investments.

CATEGORIES OF SERVICES

Within operations management, there is a fair amount of knowledge, theories, and techniques that apply, whether you are talking about goods or services. The line between a good and a service is blurred and is often represented as a continuum, as presented in Figure 4-3. Vacation "products" can be a pure service, such as a massage, or a pure good, such as a souvenir mug. Most products are a combination of good and service. Because of the intangible and experiential nature of most services, it can be a point of debate as to whether manufacturing principles and techniques are appropriate for service settings.

One way to frame the debate is to examine the service process matrix.[7] The matrix compares labor intensity (LI) with the degree of interaction and customization (IC) to categorize four different types of services:

- Low LI and low IC: service factory (such as garbage collection)
- High LI and low IC: mass services (such as retailing)
- Low LI and high IC: service shops (such as automobile repair)
- High LI and high IC: professional services (such as attorneys)

In the cases of lower interaction, or service factories and mass services, operations tend to have high capital investment and greater opportunities for applying insights from manufacturing processes. For example, in garbage collection, some service providers have standardized the gurneys they provide to residential customers, so sanitation workers can use automated lifts to

Figure 4-3   The Services-Goods Continuum: Vacation Products

PURE GOOD

Souvenir

Cappuccino

Hotel Stay

Air Travel

Massage

PURE SERVICE

dump the contents of the gurneys. The service providers can use computerized models to optimize scheduling and truck routing.

To some extent, opportunities for automation also exist for mass services, as evidenced by the use of scanners and universal product codes. However, because of the high level of labor intensity, consistency in customer interaction is a critical success factor for mass services. Efforts to achieve consistency in this type of service can be informed by manufacturing process control.

The low LI of a service shop represents the cost of labor relative to the equipment needed to provide a service. While there may not be a lot of interaction between you and your mechanic, the service provided is customized to your vehicle and is therefore considered high IC. Here the application of quality management techniques, originally developed for manufacturing, can apply.

The last category is probably the most contentious in the debate. While professionals do not like to think that they can be viewed through a manufacturing lens, an argument can be made for drawing parallels between professional services firms and flexible manufacturing systems. Thus, scheduling algorithms and "machine tooling" heuristics can be helpful.[8]

One of the most valuable approaches to come from manufacturing and be applicable to services is a technique used for NPD/NSD. It is a practical approach that can be quite useful, whether it is used casually or rigorously. Applying this technique can have a direct impact on organizational performance.

TECHNIQUE: QUALITY FUNCTION DEPLOYMENT

This approach to new product development—also called QFD—originated in Japan in the 1960s, and Xerox brought it to the United States in the mid-1980s. It is a systematic way to incorporate customers' needs and preferences into the design and development process using a series of matrices. Because of the structure of the matrices, this approach is also referred to as a house of quality (HOQ).

Like any methodology, it can be cumbersome, but when used effectively, it promotes cross-functional collaboration and a rational conversation of capabilities in the context of customer preferences. It can also provide an excellent at-a-glance view of competitive positioning, importance weights, critical process requirements, and trade-offs. QFD documents also provide a good audit trail for change management requests, allowing you to remember what a specification was in the first place and who was willing to change it.

The complete process calls for developing a series of matrices that compare the following:[9]

- Customer requirements and technical features
- Technical features and potential technologies
- Potential technologies with production processes
- Production processes with quality control
- Quality control with specifications

In this way, the process leads from what the customer wants to how you will provide it and ensure that you are doing it well. One of the reasons that QFD is a valuable technique is that the starting point is the understanding of customer requirements. These can be both solicited and unsolicited, qualitative and quantitative.

Some HOQ diagrams are simple; others are quite detailed. The matrix form enables the NPD/NSD team to capture a lot of information in one place. At a minimum, you want customer requirements noted on the left and, if possible, assigned importance ratings. Think of these as desired benefits. They are posed against technical requirements or possible features across the top of the matrix. The main part of the house includes an analysis of interrelationships between the two sets of requirements; for example, the roll thickness and tensile strength of the paper are strongly related to ensuring that the paper will not tear.

The roof of the HOQ in Figure 4-4 is an analysis of the potential synergies, meaning whether a certain technical capability helps or hinders another

Figure 4-4   Textbook House of Quality

Customer Weights	Desired "Whats"	Writing Style	Examples	Test Bank	Class Aids	MY TEXT	ACME'S TEXT
50%	Relevance	😊	😊			5	5
12%	Supplements			😊	😊	3	4
25%	Readability	😊				5	3
13%	Affordability			⊘	⊘	5	2
TARGET OR LIMIT		90% ratings ≥ very good	At least 3 per chapter	Available online	At least 4 per chapter	WEIGHTED 4.76	SCORES 3.42

KEY: 😊 Strong positive
      😊 Positive
      ⊘ Negative
      ⊘ Strong negative

technical capability. In the printing process, we can see that there is a strong negative relationship between the paper thickness and the roll roundness. Some discussion of trade-offs should ensue.

If desired, the matrix can be expanded with competitive evaluations. Those are presented in the right wing of the house. The basement can be used to capture the technical evaluation of possible options or existing products. You can see the target values and their importance weights, presumably agreed to by the development team.

Although the HOQ diagram can certainly be hand drawn, such as on a flip chart in a group meeting, templates are available online (webducate .net/?page_id=713 and http://qfdonline.com/templates).

To build our own example, consider using QFD to develop a textbook. While students are the ones who actually purchase the books and can be considered consumers, the customers are really the professors who select the textbooks. As a faculty member, my criteria for textbooks are relevance (5), supplemental resources (3), readability (4), and affordability (2). The numbers represent factor ratings in importance on a scale of 1 (low) to 5 (high). That completes the left side of the matrix.

Across the top of the matrix are the technical features, which can also be prioritized using the same scale: writing style (4), current examples (5), class exercises (4), test bank (2), and visual aids (2). The main part of the house covers which technical features address customer requirements. For example, writing style will have a very strong positive impact on readability but none on relevance. A test bank and visual aids will have a somewhat negative impact on affordability. Current examples and class exercises contribute strongly to the textbook's relevance.

In considering the synergies of the technical requirements (the roof), let's assume that current examples have a slightly negative trade-off with a test bank and visual aids because of time constraints.

Remember, QFD is just a starting point for discussion for your NPD/NSD team. As you gain consensus on each part of the matrix, you develop a sense of priorities and needs and can continue with further planning for technology selection, production process, and quality assurance. The value of the technique is not in the resulting matrices, but in going through the process. The goal should be to create a common vision and consensus about how to meet your customers' requirements.

Application and Reflection
1. What trade-offs have you experienced, either at work or as a consumer?
2. What services do you consume in each quadrant of the service matrix?

SUMMARY

New product and service development is integral to an organization's performance. It is a funnel-like process that typically progresses from idea generation to feasibility analysis and business case development. Sources of ideas can be customer-driven (market pull) or technology-driven (technology push).

Typical trade-offs in design factors include choices between product/service features, flexibility and efficiency, inventory levels and responsiveness, hiring and using overtime, and risk and reward. A key consideration in organizational performance is the total cost of ownership, which represents a trade-off between short- and long-term costs.

Product/service delivery processes typically range from a project form to a job shop, batch process, assembly line, or continuous flow, depending on the volume, level of technological investment, and life-cycle stage of the product. Service offerings can be categorized by both the labor intensity and the extent of the interaction and customization with customers.

Quality function deployment is a collaborative NPD/NSD technique that starts with customer requirements and translates them into what the product should be, how it will be produced, and how to ensure quality.

Review Questions

1. New product development can originate with a technology push or a market pull.
   a. True
   b. False

2. Feasibility analysis _____.
   a. is the last stage in NPD/NSD
   b. determines whether a product concept is viable
   c. can be done through a market research study
   d. is a requirement for dynamic stability
   e. None of the above

3. At each stage of NPD/NSD, projects are examined more closely and require more information to move into the next stage of development.
   a. True
   b. False

4. A portfolio view of a company's products means _____.
   a. products should be diversified by industry
   b. products should be diversified by life cycle
   c. products should be diversified by resource allocation
   d. b and c
   e. All of the above

5. It is best to develop a replacement product after a product starts to decline.
   a. True
   b. False

6. Product development teams help against time-based competitive pressures by _____.
   a. enabling concurrent engineering
   b. catching errors and design flaws earlier in the process
   c. leading to a more robust design
   d. a and c
   e. All of the above

7. Reverse innovation is when a company disassembles a competitor's product and figures out how to build it.
   a. True
   b. False

8. Which of the following is a typical trade-off to be decided in NPD/NSD?
   a. Short- versus long-term costs
   b. Potential benefits versus risks
   c. Carry inventory versus allow backorders
   d. b and c
   e. All of the above

9. Process designs vary by _____.
   a. potential volume of production
   b. investment in technology
   c. type of job
   d. a and b
   e. All of the above

10. A service operation that has high labor intensity and a low degree of interaction and customization for the customer is a _____.
   a. service factory
   b. mass service
   c. service shop
   d. professional service
   e. service matrix

11. Quality function deployment is a methodology to _____.
   a. compare what the customer wants and what you can do
   b. compare what the customer wants with your product's specifications
   c. compare importance weights of your competitors
   d. compare functions with features
   e. None of the above

5

QUALITY ACROSS THE ORGANIZATION

I can't define [it] . . . but I know it when I see it.
—POTTER STEWART, OPINION IN
JACOBELLIS V. OHIO (1964)

ypically, if you manage for specific results, they include improved performance and/or increased quality. In this chapter, you will learn the foundation for quality management across an organization. We will address quality in the specific contexts of processes and the management of projects in later chapters.

After completing this chapter, you should be able to do the following:

- Define *quality*
- Explain the key principles of quality management
- Compare and contrast *Six Sigma*, *lean production*, and *ISO 9000* approaches to quality

- Follow the *DMAIC* process
- Use quality management tools to perform *problem determination*

DEFINITIONS OF QUALITY

Let's first be clear about what we mean by quality. Definitions can vary by perspective, such as whether you are the customer or the producer. A producer is typically focused on meeting specifications and limiting defects. A customer-based explanation may be unstated, vague, variable, and/or subjective. It is easy to see how challenging a firm definition of *quality* can be. This is especially true in the delivery of services, when the definition can vary from customer to customer.

In his review of studies evaluating the effects of quality on business performance, Hardie identified a variety of different definitions, including "keeping the service promise; attaining a specification; meeting the customer's expectations; performing the intended functions; being free of deficiencies; comparing favorably to competitors; and minimizing variation from the ideal."[1] Each of these differs in subtle ways from the others.

A construct that is often confused with the concept of quality is *value*. Value is really a ratio of performance and price. You might stay at a five-star resort and find the service and amenities to be of outstanding quality. But if you are taking the kids on vacation, a chain with a breakfast bar and an outdoor pool might be a better value.

In this book, we will use the International Standards Organization's (ISO's) definition of *quality* in Standard 8402: "The totality of features and characteristics of a product or service that bear on its ability to satisfy stated or implied needs." This definition captures the customer perspective and notes that needs can be stated or implied. Also, it is applicable to products along the goods-services continuum described in Chapter 4.

Operationally, quality can be measured along twelve different dimensions: (1) conformance to specifications, (2) performance, (3) quick response, (4) quick-change expertise, (5) features, (6) reliability, (7) durability, (8) serviceability, (9) aesthetics, (10) perception, (11) humanity, and (12) value.[2] These dimensions are fairly self-explanatory, but it is helpful to think of specific examples. One of my favorite illustrations of measuring quality is to compare a Bic ballpoint pen to a Mont Blanc fountain pen. I would suggest that a Mont Blanc is superior according to criteria 1, 7, 8, 9, 10, and perhaps

11 (since the Bic is disposable and has a negative environmental impact); the Bic is of higher quality in terms of criteria 2 (the ink doesn't bleed, but it does clump), 6 (you can tell when it's going to run out of ink), and 12 (it is the price performer). In this example, the other dimensions of quality don't really apply.

THE QUALITY MOVEMENT IN BUSINESSES

As you might expect, being concerned about quality across the organization started in the early days of the Industrial Revolution, accelerated during World War II, and became a top priority for American business executives when Japanese products began taking higher market shares in the 1970s and 1980s. It continues to be at the top of management agendas today.

Early Proponents

One pioneer was Fredrick Taylor, known for his motion studies and standardized working motions that not only made workers more productive, but also created greater consistency in worker output. Quality was typically measured at the end of the production process; it consisted of weeding out defects and was known as *quality assurance*.

This end-of-the-line view is problematic. Not only have you wasted resources to produce unsalable products, but there are situations in which you just cannot inspect every product. Limitations can stem from the quantity of products to inspect, the time it takes to examine each one, or the fact that some testing is destructive (as in crash tests). If you are trying to improve the quality of a process, you may not be able to inspect every step in the process or easily access the necessary equipment.

Such was the impetus behind Dr. Walter Shewhart's contribution to the quality movement. As a statistician for Western Electric, he was concerned with improving the reliability of telephone transmission systems (which were often buried underground, making them costly to test or repair). He is credited with first suggesting that statistical sampling within a process is a better way to identify real problems and avoid overcorrections. Shewhart's legacy is *statistical process control* charts (which you will learn to enjoy and interpret in Chapter 8).

Shewhart mentored a physicist who was concerned with the variability of measurement errors, Dr. W. Edwards Deming. They collaborated during World War II, after which Deming introduced Shewhart's approach in Japan during the rebuilding of its manufacturing industry. Interestingly, Deming was unsuccessful in gaining the attention of American manufacturers until the 1970s, when OPEC's oil embargo made the small, fuel-efficient Japanese cars more attractive to buyers than the U.S.-made gas-guzzlers they had been buying.

Deming's contribution extended past applications of statistical process control to encompass managing quality across the organization. He developed the 14 Points for quality improvement but is arguably more renowned for his "seven deadly obstacles" to quality practices:[3]

1. Lack of constancy of purpose
2. Emphasis on short-term profits
3. Evaluation of performance (for example, management by objectives)
4. Mobility of top management
5. Running on visible figures
6. Excessive medical costs
7. Excessive cost of warranty

In addition to overcoming or avoiding the seven obstacles, the fundamental concepts underlying the 14 Points, or imperatives, are visionary leadership, internal and external cooperation, learning, process management, continuous improvement, employee fulfillment, and customer satisfaction.[4]

Another Western Electric statistician and early proponent of the need to manage quality across organizations was Joseph M. Juran. He is perhaps best known for the "quality trilogy"—the need for quality planning, control, and improvement. Planning for quality in product or process development was not a widespread practice then, and the common thinking was, "If it ain't broke, don't fix it." Juran advocated the need for continuous improvement across the organization.[5]

One other individual of note in the quality movement is Philip B. Crosby, a consultant and author who coined the popular catch phrase "Quality is free."[6] What he was really saying was that poor quality is costly when you consider the internal and external costs of defects. So even though there are costs when an organization takes measures to prevent and/or appraise defects, these expenses are offset by the savings from not having to fix defects; hence, quality is free. The types of costs are summarized in Table 5-1.[7]

The external cost of repairs is particularly poignant in the recent series of recalls by Toyota. The company has estimated the cost of the recalls to be around $2 billion (U.S.) and 100,000 units in lost sales.[8] It is unclear whether this estimate includes the time lost by executives doing damage control and engineers developing ways to correct the underlying problems.

The complexity of recalls can be staggering, especially when you consider high-volume consumer goods. First, the quality problem has to be detected, usually catastrophically and repeatedly, somewhere in the value chain. The source of the problem has to be isolated. It may be difficult to diagnose for any of a number of reasons, such as having several different suppliers for a suspect input, needing to search complex manufacturing lines and material handling conduits for a contaminant, or experiencing intermittent problems in a range of applications or usage environments. Once the problem

Table 5-1   The Costs of Quality

Prevention Costs	Appraisal Costs	Internal Costs	External Costs
Employee training	Inspection and testing of products	Scrap and rework	Warranty repairs
Process capability studies	Capital cost and ongoing maintenance of inspection and testing equipment	Charges related to late payments	Field service personnel training
Surveys of vendors, suppliers, and subcontractors		Inventory costs to allow for defective products	Complaint handling
	Cost to process and report inspection data	Engineering change costs for design correction	Customer dissatisfaction
	Design reviews	Premature failure of products	Future business losses
	Expense reviews	Correction of documentation	Litigation

is identified, remediation options must be considered from a technical and a financial (and hopefully, an ethical) perspective. Of course, this is before the actual recall is performed.

Even when the recall is not a recall, as in the recent case of Nestlē's refrigerated cookie dough, when consumers were advised to discard packages of refrigerated dough because of risks of *E. coli* infection,[9] it can be a costly and cumbersome operation. Under prevention costs, Nestlē had to investigate the source of contamination and take measures to eliminate it. In addition, there was likely a cost to relabel products to warn consumers not to consume raw dough. For appraisal costs, additional testing throughout the supply chain was necessary. In terms of rework costs, 300,000 cases of the product were discarded, representing lost revenue. The external costs of illnesses, deaths, and lawsuits are remarkable. Damage to the company's public relations is likely but difficult to measure.

Business Applications

In the 1980s, companies started putting the pieces together—first in Japan and then in the United States—into an organizational development effort known as *total quality management* (TQM). The idea of "total" implied the involvement of the entire organization and required *teamwork*.[10] For example, the customer became the next person in the production process. Paired with the motto "Do the right thing right the first time," the philosophy enabled workers to detect errors earlier in the production process and empowered them to correct them.

Another key principle behind TQM was the emphasis on a *customer focus*, with the understanding that consistent customer satisfaction could be attained only through *continuous improvement*, which required collaboration throughout the organization.[11] Improvements might be cost reductions, productivity increases, or competitive superiority.[12] The bottom line for TQM was increased profits.

To promote TQM practices and national competitiveness, the U.S. government established the Malcolm Baldrige National Quality Award in 1988. Baldrige examiners would evaluate an organization in the following categories: leadership, information and analysis, strategic quality planning, human resource utilization, quality assurance of products and services, quality results, and customer satisfaction. While winning the award is still generally viewed as prestigious, it is no guarantor of financial success, as evidenced by the financial problems Federal Express experienced after receiving it.[13]

As with many other organizational development initiatives, despite widespread awareness and pursuit of TQM in the corporate world, efforts often stalled and, in some cases, failed. From what I have read and experienced, I believe the lack of success stories stemmed largely from partial implementations, lackluster executive support, and unclear expectations. I also think TQM was often confused with ISO 9000, a certification standard set by the International Standards Organization.

The 9000 series of standards call for identifying and documenting processes, making provisions for continuous improvement (such as feedback loops), and satisfying customer specifications. The ISO 9000 certification is often a requirement for suppliers, largely in Europe and in the U.S. auto industry. As many a Dilbert cartoon has implied, however, you can end up with a lot of paper that may or may not lead to the desired quality across an organization. The costs can outweigh the benefits of certification.[14] In addition, it is important to understand the following points about ISO 9000:[15]

- It is not interchangeable with quality management.
- It is compatible with, and can be a subset of, quality management.
- It is frequently implemented in a non–quality management environment.
- It can improve operations in a traditional environment.
- It may be redundant in a mature quality management environment.

Widely accepted now, the ISO 9000 certification generally provides suppliers with competitive parity rather than an advantage.

SIX SIGMA

As the TQM movement declined, it was replaced by Six Sigma practices. The original term for *Six Sigma* was coined by an engineer at Motorola in 1986 as a way to standardize the way defects were tallied and process quality was defined. By specifying that defects cannot occur within six standard deviations (a.k.a. sigma, or σ) from the process mean, *Six Sigma* implies very few defects, or 3.4 defects per million opportunities (*DPMO*). If you hear the term used today, however, that is probably not what it means.

As a noun, *Six Sigma* refers to a disciplined, organization-wide system that replaced TQM. I think of it as TQM version 2.0, with a clear set of processes, defined roles and responsibilities, and a broader view of the value chain (from suppliers to customers). The objective is still the same: to meet or exceed customer needs through company-wide continuous improvement, which should lead to profits on the bottom line.

In their book, *Leading Six Sigma*, Snee and Hoerl examine successful and not-so-successful implementations of Six Sigma. In addition to the principles and success factors already discussed, they emphasize the need for process (systems) thinking, the value of data-based decisions, and the effect of variability in undermining quality across the organization.[16] We see again the importance of a systems view of an operation.

In my opinion, the specific aspects that have made Six Sigma more effective than TQM are the formalization of roles, a defined methodology, and a specified toolkit. In the formalization of roles, a leadership team (LT) is responsible for the overall implementation of Six Sigma. The LT members are involved in project selection and review, and they communicate the priority and progress of each initiative throughout the organization. They also ensure that project leaders have adequate training and preparation for their responsibilities.

Quality improvements are achieved through a series of projects. These projects involve giving staff defined roles, such as champions, who are typically members of the LT who "block and tackle" for the project leaders. Project leaders are typically ranked by "belts"—green, black, and master black belts (MBBs)—in increasing order of technical ability and project experience. A green belt will lead a smaller project than a black belt, for example.

The projects generally follow a specified methodology, known as DMAIC for the five phases of the project: define, measure, analyze, improve, and control. Each phase has specific tools associated with it. (This methodology is really the scientific method used in a business research framework, as we saw in Chapter 2.) Within each phase, specific techniques are considered part of the Six Sigma toolkit.

The define phase of a DMAIC project focuses on clearly specifying the problem or opportunity, what the goals are for the process improvement project, and what the scope of the project is. To pursue opportunities, you might find quality function deployment (see Chapter 4) used here. Another useful technique is benchmarking, which involves comparing an organization's processes with the best practices to be found in the field. Benchmarking can be done internally (such as comparing regional offices' sales production), against a competitor (such as comparing the impact of advertising campaigns on market share), or with a noncompetitor (such as comparing a department store's customer service training with existing training for an oil-change franchise). At the end of this chapter, you will learn a few of the simple techniques that can be helpful for problem determination and usually require a lot of discussion but not a lot of calculation.

The measure phase begins with the identification of the key process performance metrics (see Chapter 3). Once those metrics have been specified, related process and customer data are collected. One of the best sources of data is customer complaints, which may be categorized and counted in this phase.

In the analysis phase, the objective is to utilize the data that have been collected in order to develop and test theories related to the root causes of existing gaps between the process's current performance and its desired performance. The analysis may be quantitative or qualitative, depending on the data. It is important to consider a wide range of possibilities.

Once a course of action has been decided upon based on the data and the analyses performed, the project moves into the improvement phase. Typically the improvement will follow what Deming called the Shewhart cycle, or plan-do-check-act (*PDCA*). The implementation of the improvement should be planned carefully, so as to minimize disruptions to existing operations and customers. Once the improvement is done, it is important to check its effect. If all is well and under control, then the next step is to close down the project and move on to another initiative. If, however, the change does not have the desired effect, it may be necessary to make adjustments or to try another approach.

The final phase, control, is the focus of Chapter 8. It is important to understand that *control* does not mean "keep things the same." The spirit of continuous improvement is critical to successfully implementing Six Sigma.

LEAN PRODUCTION

Another approach to quality across the organization, particularly in manufacturing facilities is known as *lean production* and follows the Toyota Production System (*TPS*), developed by the car manufacturer in Japan. Central to the TPS philosophy is the elimination of all forms of *waste*, including those related to time. Waste is considered the use of resources that do not add value in the eyes of the customer.

Waste is often classified into one of the following seven categories: overproduction, inventory, waiting, unnecessary transport, unnecessary processing, unnecessary human motions, and defects.[17]

In examining a lean transformation system, activities are considered value-added (for example, making a patient diagnosis); non-value-added but necessary (such as requiring patients to sign a privacy form); or non-value-added and unnecessary (as in waiting for the doctor). This is consistent with the practical approach and a systems view of the operational system, described in Chapter 2.

Another characteristic of lean production is the direction of the flow. As opposed to the "make to inventory" approach of "pushing" materials through a plant, lean enterprises rely on pull systems, whereby actual customer demand drives the production process. A pull system is a control-based system that signals the requirement for parts just as they are needed, hence it is called *just-in-time* (*JIT*). It starts with a customer order, involves close ties with suppliers, and accommodates little variability in the production process.

The beauty of a JIT pull system (also known as in Japanese as *Kanban*) is that it reduces all inventory levels, improves process and product quality, and further eliminates waste. The challenge is that high inventory hides process and material problems, so moving to JIT can be painful, because those problems are uncovered. It is similar to the metaphor of a ship sailing in deep water over rocks. As the tide goes out and the water (inventory) level goes down, the ship (company) is in more shallow water and runs into the rocks (problems).

Five tools lean organizations commonly turn to in their pursuit of perfection are *5S*, the *visual factory, poka yokes, kaizen* (or continuous improvement), and *total productive maintenance*.[18] Let's explore each of these lean tools in more detail, as they have broad applicability beyond the manufacturing environment.

5S stands for "sort, straighten (or set in order), scrub (shine), systematize, and standardize (sustain)." Lean organizations are very neat. Everything has its place. Is that true in your office? Your kitchen? You can apply the 5S approach almost anywhere. For instance, we have a wonderful franchise in town called Super Suppers (supersuppers.com) that exemplifies 5S. Every month, it offers a new menu of a dozen different dinners. Staff will prepare them for you if you like, but it is a joy to go there and "make dinner." Each recipe is clearly posted at a specified workstation (sort). The ingredients for that recipe are kept in neat bins on a cold table, with the appropriate measuring spoon or cup next to the associated ingredient (set in order). The place is immaculate (shine); the process is easy to follow (systematize); and the experience is consistent month after month (standardize).

Building on the 5S tool, a *visual factory* adds the element of visual cues and signage. Problems can be identified through the use of charts displayed throughout the workplace. Not only does this help to make problems visible, but regular postings can help employees stay up-to-date on current operating conditions. Signage is often used to communicate process improvement goals. Designating specific places to store tools—such as with outlines on wall-mounted Peg-Board or tape marks on the floor for larger items—makes it clear where things are to be located. This saves time on storage, search, and retrieval.

Poka yokes, or fail-safes, are one of my favorite techniques. They are proactive in that they are designed to prevent errors. A *poka yoke* can be a warning that signals the existence of a problem, a precautionary measure to prevent a problem from occurring, or a control that stops production until the problem is resolved.[19] You likely have experienced one type of poka yoke: a data mask will not allow invalid or incorrect data, such as incorrect product codes, to be entered into a computer system. A more tangible example is the need to have your foot on the brake to shift your car out of park or the need for the car to be in park to remove the key from the ignition.

Sometimes, a fail-safe measure is not really "fail" safe, such as we have seen with the oil drill operated by British Petroleum in the Gulf of Mexico, where the prevention mechanism did not operate as intended. Poka yoke failures are not always mechanical in nature; recently, *The Wall Street Journal* reported that medication errors cause at least one death every day. Part of the problem stems from similar packaging being used for completely disparate drugs. Attempts to establish fail-safes for some drugs in dropper bottles by using color coding have apparently exacerbated the confusion, because color-coding bottles has made items within each product class harder to differentiate. Bar codes and electronic medical records may be the best way to "eliminate the danger of illegible handwritten orders and have programs to automatically question drugs or doses that don't match up with a patient's age, condition, or diagnosis. And bar-coding systems require drugs to be scanned . . . as an automatic check that the prescribed drug is the one being administered at the bedside."[20]

When implementing fail-safes in services, you must account for customer errors as well as for server errors: "Server errors can be . . . errors in the task, the treatment, or the tangible aspects of service, while customer errors can be classified as errors in the preparation for the encounter, the encounter, or the resolution of the encounter."[21]

For example, think of a dry-cleaning establishment where you have clothes laundered and pressed. On the server side, an error in the task might be miscounting the number of shirts in the order. A treatment error could be the wrong amount of starch on the collars. A tangible aspect going wrong may be the shirts becoming crushed and wrinkled when they are wrapped and stored for pickup. On the customer side, an error in the preparation for the encounter might be failing to highlight a stain that needs special treatment. An error in the encounter might be to forget to pick up the receipt or to drive away without the clean clothes. The resolution of the encounter can go awry when a customer becomes angry and accusatory, such as when a garment is perceived as missing.

Poka yokes try to prevent such errors. Think of pumping gas into your car: you cannot make a mistake and use leaded gasoline or diesel, because those nozzles will not fit your car's gas tank (preparation for the encounter). Some poka yokes are really creative. I recently learned of video games being projected in urinals to improve men's "encounter."[22]

Kaizen, a Japanese term for "change for the better," represents the philosophy of continuous improvement. This is integral to any quality management system. You need to actively seek ways to improve the operation. Sometimes, one of the best improvements you can make is to achieve consistency.

Consistency can have life-or-death consequences. In his book *The Checklist Manifesto*, Dr. Atul Gawande explains how a humble checklist can improve outcomes in operating rooms. He has developed one for the incredibly complex field of surgery that takes 90 seconds to complete. With its use in eight different hospitals, the checklist has arguably reduced complications and deaths by more than 33 percent—at virtually no cost. As Dr. Gawande explains, "In a complex environment, experts are up against two main difficulties. The first is the fallibility of the human memory and attention, especially when it comes to mundane, routine matters that are easily overlooked . . . [The second] is that people can lull themselves into skipping steps even when they remember them. . . . Checklists seem to provide protection against such failures. They remind us of the minimum necessary steps and make them explicit."[23]

Total productive maintenance (*TPM*) is a proactive measure to avoid the wastes incurred by equipment breakdowns or other stoppages. The idea is to maximize equipment availability without wasting other resources. Coordinating engineering, operations, and maintenance work is crucial. Perhaps you apply TPM to your automobile. Isn't it more convenient to have the oil changed and the tires rotated at periodic, planned intervals than to have the car break down or a tire blow out while you are driving?

Clearly, the techniques used in Six Sigma and lean production are applicable to operations management for services, since these can also benefit from waste removal, variability reduction, improved flexibility, and increased responsiveness. Snee and Hoerl have described the improvements experienced by General Electric's corporate audit staff, a finance function, as a result of implementing Six Sigma; they include the following:[24]

- Reducing the average and variability of days outstanding for accounts receivable (collecting money faster)
- Improving the audit process to be more accurate (having fewer missed issues) and faster
- Improving the acquisition process (performing faster with fewer resources and fewer mistakes)
- Reducing variation in cash flow (improving financial management and forecasting)
- Improving payroll accuracy, including deductions for taxes and benefits (reducing complaints and corrections)

Quality practices such as JIT and lean principles are also applicable to project management:

In a project environment, it is most desirable for the materials and components to arrive at the precise time of need rather than several days or weeks ahead of the need date. Early arrival of large bulk materials often causes problems with storage space as well as the potential for deterioration through weather or loss through pilferage. Climate-sensitive equipment requires controlled environmental storage. All these items add cost to a project and increase the risk.[25]

Common to all of these practices, whether you are dealing with an assembly-line operation, a continuous flow process, or a service environment, is a focus on the customer, collaboration within the organization, emphasis on continuous improvement, elimination of variability, and identification of value and waste.

TECHNIQUE: QUALITY MANAGEMENT TOOLS

By the time you complete this course, you should be fully equipped to achieve quality across your organization—whether it is a department, a small business, or a corporation. You already understand the need to examine your operation as a system and how to measure for results. In later chapters, we will cover process design, analysis, and control, as well as the project management concepts and techniques you will need to implement improvements using the DMAIC methodology of Six Sigma.

For now, let's talk about some basic quality tools that are particularly useful for problem determination, measurement, and preliminary analysis—the first three phases of DMAIC. For illustration purposes, imagine that you are the plant manager for a manufacturing facility. The throughput of your plant (the rate at which new products are produced) is unsatisfactory. That is a problem, but it is not a problem definition. The TPS suggests using a technique called the 5 Whys, where you work backward from the effect to the cause by asking, "Why?" (http://mind tools.com). In our illustration, your questions might look something like this:

1. **Why is our throughput unsatisfactory?** Because the equipment is down too often.
2. **Why is the equipment down?** Because it is taking too long to change over lines for different product runs.

3. **Why is it taking too long?** Because the maintenance team is fumbling for their tools.
4. **Why are they fumbling?** Because tools are often in the wrong place in the shop.
5. **Why are they in the wrong place?** Because we don't have enough of a few key wrenches, so the maintenance technicians have a hard time tracking down the tools they need.

As you can see, the 5 Whys encourage you to drill down to a root cause and can help you define the problem. Since quality management practices call for data-based decision making, you ask the manufacturing manager to measure the problem by keeping track of the outages. A simple numerical count of the different types of causes is the most appropriate metric at this point, so she records the causes for the delay in their resolution. To collect the data, she uses a check sheet like the one shown in Table 5-2, which lists possible causes. (If she has overlooked a possibility, she can simply add it to the list when it occurs.)

For the next 10 outages that seem to take longer than they should, she talks with the maintenance team to determine what is causing the delay. In her analysis, she determines that the problem is not missing tools as much as missing parts that are needed (such as blades, drills, clamps, and spare parts). The *Pareto principle*, also known as the 80/20 rule, suggests that 80 percent of problems are caused by 20 percent of possible causes. From the check sheet, it looks like solving the problem of the missing parts will alleviate many of the delays.

Table 5-2 A Check Sheet Example

Possible Cause	Frequency
Missing tools	|
Staffing shortage	|
Missing parts	///// |
Reworking changeover	||

So the manufacturing manager meets with other people in the plant, including the spare parts inventory supervisor, the maintenance chief, and a line supervisor to brainstorm possible causes. The brainstorming approach requires that participants follow certain rules:

- Withhold judgment about suggested ideas
- Express all ideas no matter how radical, unconventional, or impractical they may seem
- Generate as many ideas as possible
- Combine and extend on one another's ideas

A climate of trust and camaraderie helps the brainstorming process a great deal. In this case, the team decides to implement visual factory concepts and mark clearly designated bins for parts to be kept at the appropriate workstations. The manager will continue to inspect the situation to ensure that it is under control.

For an example that applies to a service operation, suppose that a local bookstore has experienced flat sales. While this could be caused by many things, the owner has the feeling that customer complaints have increased over the past few months. Going back through old message slips, feedback cards, and scribbled notes, he finds that the complaints fall into four major categories: missing books, loud customers, restroom issues, and other. He does not know which issue he should tackle first.

Sometimes it can help to graph the data, especially if you have a lot of data points. A *Pareto chart*, which demonstrates the 80/20 rule, looks like a bar chart but has some key differences. As you can see from Figure 5-1, the bars are arranged in decreasing order of frequency, with a line indicating the cumulative distribution above the bars. Traditionally, the bars are touching (which is not true of a regular bar chart).

In this case, it is easy to see that missing books are the main complaint, accounting for almost 75 percent of the issues. Solving the underlying issue—*why* the books are missing—will resolve most of the issues customers complain about. The bookstore owner pulls together his supervisors and long-time staff after hours to brainstorm about the problem.

One way to generate and capture ideas from this session is to use a *cause-and-effect diagram*; Figure 5-2 gives an example of what the brainstorming team may have produced. Also known as a *fishbone diagram*

Figure 5-1   Sample Pareto Chart: Bookstore Customer Complaints

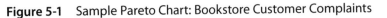

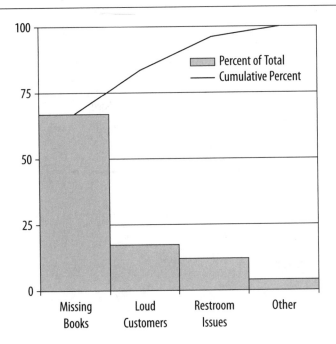

because of its shape, the technique was developed by Tenichi Ishikawa. To elicit possible causes, you might find it helpful to use a category mnemonic— men, machines, materials, methods, measurement, and miscellaneous—to elicit suggestions from your team. With a thorough list of possible causes, the team may agree to collect more data to investigate the key causes further. They continue through the DMAIC process until satisfied that the appropriate resolution has been reached.

   Please note that in problem definition you often have to consider the impact of time. For example, a *run chart* plots counts or measures (*y*-axis) against time (*x*-axis), meaning in sequential order. This might help to identify trends or cycles in the data. Segmenting the data in a *bar graph*, by shift, can also be edifying. The time you invest in defining the problem correctly will pay dividends when you are able to find the right solution in a timely manner.

Figure 5-2   Sample Fishbone Diagram: Missing Books

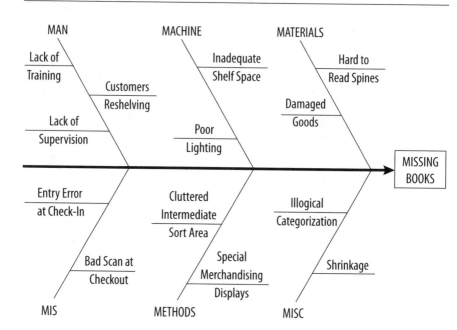

Application and Reflection
1. Think of an example for each of the quality dimensions where that dimension is critical for a quality result.
2. How and what would you benchmark if you were the manager of an accounting department, a bank branch office, a hotel front desk, or a corporate website?
3. What fail-safe measures have you encountered?

SUMMARY

Quality is defined as the totality of features and characteristics of a product or service that bear on its ability to satisfy stated or implied needs.

The basic principles for managing quality across an organization are to focus on the customer, promote teamwork and empowerment within the organization, emphasize continuous improvement, identify value added and waste, and reduce variability. Six Sigma, lean production, and total quality management are all management systems used to improve quality across the organization. They follow the same basic principles and employ many of the same techniques in implementation. The ISO 9000 standards also pertain to management across the organization, but they are more of an evaluation and certification tool than an implementation approach.

The use of 5S, visual factory, poka yokes, kaizen, and TPM can reduce the waste in any operation. Waste can stem from overproduction, inventory, wait time, unnecessary transport, unnecessary processing, unnecessary human motions, and defects. One simple way to improve consistency in an operation (thereby reducing defects) is to use process checklists.

The DMAIC methodology used in Six Sigma is a variation on the scientific method used in systems thinking; it uses the phases of define, measure, analyze, inspect, and control to execute improvement projects. Simple tools such as check sheets, Pareto charts, cause-and-effect diagrams, run charts, and bar charts can be useful in problem determination.

Review Questions

1. There is only one correct way to define quality.
   a. True
   b. False
2. Value is a measure of the price for performance of a product.
   a. True
   b. False
3. Quality is defined as the totality of product characteristics to satisfy customers' needs.
   a. True
   b. False

4. Which of the following is *not* a dimension by which quality can be measured?
   a. Features
   b. Quick-change expertise
   c. Variation from the ideal
   d. Humanity
   e. All of the above are measures of quality.

5. Match the following quality pioneer with his contribution to the quality movement.

   a. Deming   1. Statistical process control
   b. Shewhart   2. Planning for quality
   c. Crosby   3. Costs of poor quality
   d. Juran   4. Seven deadly obstacles

6. Which of the following are *not* costs of quality?
   a. Prevention costs
   b. Appraisal costs
   c. Internal costs
   d. External costs
   e. All of the above are costs of quality.

7. Which of the following are key principles of quality management?
   a. If it's not broke, don't fix it.
   b. The customer is the next person in the process.
   c. It takes everyone in the company to achieve quality.
   d. a and b
   e. b and c

8. Which of the following is a difference between quality management and ISO 9000 certification?
   a. ISO 9000 certification provides a competitive advantage.
   b. Quality management focuses on continuous improvement.
   c. ISO 9000 certification requires process documentation.
   d. ISO 9000 certification is free.
   e. ISO 9000 is interchangeable with quality management.

9. A Six Sigma quality management program implementation includes which of the following?
   a. The designation of a leadership team
   b. The use of the DMAIC methodology
   c. The purchase of belts for newly trained employees
   d. a and b
   e. All of the above

10. Tools for problem determination and preliminary analysis include which of the following?
   a. Poka yokes
   b. Pareto charts
   c. Fishbone diagrams
   d. b and c
   e. All of the above

6

TECHNOLOGY ACROSS THE VALUE CHAIN

In the technology industry people always overesti-
mate what you can do in one year and underestimate
what you do in one decade.

—MARC BENIOFF, FOUNDER AND
CEO, SALESFORCE.COM

After examining organizational performance and quality programs, we have one more major topic to cover at the organizational level before we get into the nitty-gritty of processes
and projects. Often integral to the competitive strategies of an
organization, technology is a critical resource in operations
and can affect the organization's ability to compete on the basis of cost, time,
quality, and/or flexibility.

Because technology advances so quickly, the purpose of this chapter is
not to provide details of specific technologies; that information is perishable.
To be an effective operations manager, you should have a deep awareness
and understanding of the three different types of technologies relevant to

your operation. It is also important to understand the potential impact of information technologies and their use in enterprise-wide systems to improve operational effectiveness.

After completing this chapter, you should be able to do the following:

- Distinguish between the different roles of technology in a value chain
- Describe the actual and potential impact of technology for an operation
- Provide examples of how *information technology* is enabling new organizational processes
- Differentiate among the key enterprise-wide information systems
- Apply the concept of a *maturity model* to evaluate an organization's capabilities

ROLES OF TECHNOLOGY

While the term *technology* is often used to describe information systems and devices, we take a broader and more fundamental view in which technology is defined as "the physical manifestation of knowledge." It is a tangible way to apply capabilities and understanding to the transformation function. Technology can be knowledge manifest in a product, process, or information system; a combination of any two; or all three. For example, e-commerce is both information technology *and* process technology. A digital entertainment system is a combination of information technology and product technology. The Kindle reading device sold by Amazon.com is an example of the convergence of all three; it is an information technology that is sold as a product and enables different reading and purchasing processes. Think of the roles of technology in terms of a Venn diagram, as shown in Figure 6-1, rather than in terms of mutually exclusive categories.

The diagram illustrates the "Venn of technology" in three separate industries. First, in polymer production, a product technology might be a particular chemical composition; a process technology could be an automated scale; and information technology might capture research data. A molecular simulation software system would be a convergence of process and information technologies.

In the second example, which addresses hair salons, hair dyes represent both process and product technologies. Shampoo is simply a product technology, and self-sharpening scissors might be an applicable process technology. Information technology could be used to capture sales receipts.

Figure 6-1   Different Roles of Technology

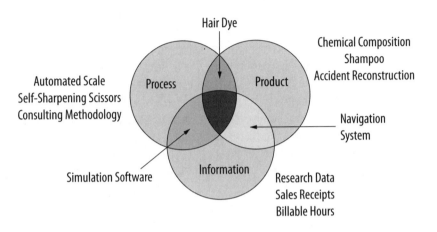

Engineering consulting firms are the third illustration. A methodology or procedure for accident investigation would be a process technology. Accident reconstruction using exemplars would be product technology. In this case, information technology captures billable hours. A combination of technologies might also be leveraged in a geographical navigation system that is used to develop a graphical reconstruction—a combination of product and information technologies.

As information technologies such as microchips continue to become faster, smaller, and less expensive, they are being integrated into more and more products. Consider how a telephone has changed over the past 30 years from a hardwired, wall-mounted device with a rotary dial to a wireless personal information system/camera/music player/Internet portal that also makes telephone calls. Managers of a well-run organization continually ask, "How can we leverage information to improve our product and service?" With the convergence of information technologies with product and process technologies, the opportunities are almost limitless.

Kelly describes microchips that are so pervasive they are called "popcorn" and foresees their use as clothing labels to tell washing machines how to care for the garments.[1] Already, we have grocery carts that can help you with your shopping:

> The [grocery cart] solution will enable anonymous ad targeting through data obtained through [the] customer loyalty card program. A shopper would scan his or her card at the [cart], and receive ads and promotional offers based on past purchases and/or saved shopping lists that could be uploaded from a home PC. No personally identifiable information will be shared. . . . The technology will also provide . . . reporting and analytics capabilities to assess performance of the ads in the stores. . . . In addition to the advertising shoppers will receive, they will also be able to save time and money . . . by obtaining electronic coupons, locating products in the store, performing comparative price checks, viewing store specials in aisles as they shop, viewing recipes and nutritional information, shopping using an electronic shopping list that is presented in aisle order, totaling the cost of the items in their baskets before checkout, and expediting the checkout using the cart-level checkout feature.[2]

It is easy to see how wireless phones can provide similar localized, targeted content. Recently, a television show built a mystery plotline around a cellular-based dating service. If two service subscribers were in the same vicinity, the service would send each person's photograph to the other's telephone and give both of them the option to connect with or reject the other person.

Sensors and information technologies are integral to process improvement in both manufacturing and services because they perform process control and measurement. Information about operating conditions, machine speeds, transaction sizes, and problem warning signs can be automated. Scanners and bar codes enable the automation of data entry and product tracking, as we experience daily in supermarkets and mass merchandising chains. Magnetic strips provide similar ease in card processing for security access, credit and debit card purchases, and employee timekeeping.

Location tracking may also be of interest to an operations manager. In the logistics industry, radio frequency identification (*RFID*) tags are used to track resources and shipments. Companies might use such data for status updates or as a security precaution. For example, to address the problems with counterfeit drugs in the pharmaceuticals industry, RFID can be used to authenticate the pedigree of the drugs with a chain-of-custody record.

With the increasing emphasis on improving sustainability and decreasing the ecological impact of operations, process technologies that monitor and control energy use are becoming crucial. It is possible to have home appliances monitor and regulate energy consumption. On a much larger scale, those capabilities are of use in both the private and public sectors.

Consider that the U.S. Department of Energy (DOE) has been charged with upgrading the nation's electrical infrastructure (called "the grid"). In the short term, the DOE is working to develop a smarter grid, one that delivers current levels of service at a lower cost and with less environmental impact. Longer term, "the Smart Grid will be characterized by a two-way flow of electricity and information and will be capable of monitoring everything from power plants to customer preferences to individual appliances. It incorporates into the grid the benefits of distributed computing and communications to deliver real-time information and enable the near-instantaneous balance of supply and demand at the device level."[3] (It is astonishing to think that these changes will occur while the grid is operating.)

In Chapter 3, you learned that you cannot manage what you do not measure. The corollary to that is that you cannot analyze what you do not capture. Information is critical to managing for results. The challenge is to leverage the appropriate technologies in a way that improves organizational performance. Too often, managers underestimate the impact technology can have on them and their operations, not least of which is *information overload.* Capturing actionable, timely data is the key. Wherever possible, managers should have information that allows them to manage by exception—that is, to identify when something is wrong and action must be taken.

TECHNOLOGY IMPACT

Beyond providing the basis for continuous improvement, information technologies can have far-reaching effects. By overcoming the need for organizations and/or individuals to be located in the same time and space, the impact of these technologies on business includes the following:

- Creating access and immediacy, which enables businesses to reach customers, suppliers, and employees anytime, anywhere
- Driving and enabling globalization, thus intensifying the competitive pressures against and heightening the social expectations of businesses of all sizes
- Changing organizational and industry structures, which facilitates outsourcing, consolidation, and dynamic collaborations
- Transforming work and careers, creating pressure on individuals to continually upgrade their capabilities to remain employable

These points emphasize that technology is a double-edged sword with the potential for positive and negative effects. Anytime/anywhere access can have unintended consequences, such as having only "virtual vacations" and losing individual privacy. Immediacy can create problems with errors that are hard to undo.[4] As Owen notes, "For 200 years, technology has been transforming society and work. Wave after wave of innovation has changed lives and changed the way we work. The pace of innovation is unlikely to slow down. The challenge for managers is to keep pace."[5]

The challenge is also for managers to anticipate what effects a technology can have on their organization. A useful framework for understanding the impact of technology was suggested by Sproull and Kiesler, in which they distinguish between first- and second-level effects.[6] First-level effects include productivity improvements and are fairly easy to quantify. For example, a company might offer 24/7 ordering capabilities through the Internet or an instructor might use a course management system to deliver class content. Second-level effects are considered social effects in that the technology changes how people and/or organizations interrelate. This is much harder to quantify, but it is evidenced in the disintermediation of wholesalers, the creation of "infomediaries" (information intermediaries), and the phenomena of viral marketing and social networks.

As we begin to shift our focus from the organization to the process level, Davenport and Short's early work on *business process reengineering* can be a good reference. They suggest that IT has the potential to do many things:

- Transform unstructured processes into routine transactions, such as making a payment or balance inquiry through an automated response system
- Transfer information rapidly and easily across large distances, making processes independent of geography, such as when U.S. tax returns are completed by accountants in India
- Replace or reduce human labor in a process, as evidenced by automated teller machines (ATMs)
- Bring complex analytical methods to bear on a process, such as mining scanner data to identify consumer purchasing behavior patterns
- Bring vast amounts of detailed information into a process, such as using the global positioning system (GPS) capability on your cellular phone to identify the closest yoga studio

- Enable changes in the sequence of tasks in a process, often allowing multiple tasks to be worked on simultaneously, as illustrated by computer-aided design and manufacturing systems
- Allow the capture and dissemination of knowledge and expertise to improve a process, as when Netflix suggests movies you might like based on your past ratings and rental history
- Allow the detailed tracking of task status, inputs, and outputs, as we do when we are waiting for a package to be delivered via UPS or Federal Express
- Connect two parties within a process that would otherwise communicate through an intermediary (internal or external), as when Dell Computer offered consumers the ability to order their computers directly from them[7]

Applicable in both manufacturing and service contexts, these insights are even more valid as information technology advances, as we will see in the following section.

APPLICATIONS OF TECHNOLOGY ACROSS AND BEYOND THE ORGANIZATION

When you apply the potential of technology, the concepts of quality management, and a systems view of the organization, it is easy to see why so many companies are pursuing integrated systems for *supply chain management, enterprise resource planning, customer relationship management*, and *knowledge management*. However, such enterprise-wide systems can be very complex and costly. The extent of organizational changes can be intractable, putting implementation at risk.

Supply Chain Management

Conceptually, *supply chain management (SCM)* encompasses the acquisition, supply, storage, and movement of materials and information across the transformation system. The idea is to coordinate and integrate all of these activities into a seamless flow. While SCM does not technically have to be computerized, as a practical matter, it is. However, the sophistication of the computerization can vary greatly—from stand-alone, PC-based applications and customized one-to-one telephone linkages to integrated databases with real-time tracking of order status.

After all, the boundaries between organizations are man-made and therefore artificial, so tight linkages with strong information capture in an SCM application can enable organizations to plan, coordinate, and collaborate as a single system. This is typically achieved through a progression of stages: coordinating parts of the internal supply chain, then combining the internal parts into an integrated solution, followed by collaborating with components of the upstream and downstream supply chain.[8] Ultimately, the goal is to integrate the entire process of satisfying the customer's needs all along the supply chain. Good SCM can provide better responsiveness, less waste, and reduced variability in the overall transformation process.

An operations manager relies heavily on an SCM system in a manufacturing environment, particularly for information about inbound and outbound *logistics*. This manager would routinely make queries such as "When are key direct materials arriving? Will there be enough storage space in the warehouse to stage the finished goods? Which carrier will pick them up for transport and when?" This information helps with scheduling resources and fulfilling orders on a timely basis.

Enterprise Resource Planning

As comprehensive as SCM is, typical SCM systems are only concerned with the flow of information and goods. *Enterprise resource planning (ERP)* further integrates functional areas with common data in a shared database management system. Typically implemented in modules that may or may not include SCM functions, ERP can encompass several types of information:

- Financial and accounting
- Human resource and payroll
- Customer
- Production

This approach provides the ability to customize each department's view of the database information—employees can see, revise, or enter only the data needed for their work.

Such systems are compelling for two reasons. First, having an integrated database management system can greatly improve data access, reliability, and currency. Be advised, though, that getting to an integrated database can create some serious turf wars while you are deciding who has what rights to which information.

Second, ERP modules are presented as best practices for organizations' business processes. The developers have benchmarked these processes, so many of the ERP screens and data structures are predefined (but customizable) for the buyer. This typically introduces a tremendous amount of organizational change, a costly amount of programming changes, or both.

Installing an ERP system is almost always challenging, taking more time and money than expected. Typically, delays and cost escalations arise from overcustomization of purchased packages and the difficulty of interfacing them with existing legacy systems.[9] Consulting firm IT Cortex reported a 2001 survey in which the companies surveyed had, or were in the process of having, completed an ERP implementation. Of those, 51 percent viewed their ERP implementation as unsuccessful. In another 2001 study referenced by IT Cortex, executives at 117 companies that had implemented ERP systems were interviewed. In this sample, 40 percent of the projects failed to achieve their business case within one year of conversion, and companies that did achieve benefits said it took six months longer than expected.[10]

ERP systems, while risky, can have a strong positive impact on a business. They can facilitate the alignment of an operation to an organization's strategy as well as enable faster reaction times to business events. For the operations manager, an ERP can help schedule employees, record time worked, determine when supplies should be reordered, and flag special instructions for individual customers. Because of the interface with financial systems, the ERP can provide quick and easy access to operational costs. Modules such as business process management, forecasting, project management, production planning, and quality management can be useful whether an organization produces goods or services. In addition, some ERP systems have modules specifically designed for services management.

Customer Relationship Management

At the other end of the value chain from suppliers and SCM—and often offered as an extension of ERP—is *customer relationship management (CRM)*. Still an integrated and comprehensive system like ERP, CRM is more specifically targeted at collecting and interpreting customer-oriented data: order history, payment history, special pricing information, contact records, complaint resolutions, and key names. A salesperson might rely on a CRM system to keep track of open items for a customer, a sales executive might evaluate that customer for cross-selling opportunities, and a financial analyst might evaluate the account's profitability. A good CRM system supports an organization's customer service, multiple channels, customer segmentation, predictive modeling, marketing integration, and performance measurement efforts.[11]

Visibility into a customer's history can provide useful information when managing operations. If some customers are more valuable to the organization, for example, their orders or service requests may be given higher priority—or not, as the following example indicates.

Sometimes a CRM system will indicate that a customer is more trouble than it is worth. "Marketplace," produced by American Public Media and broadcast by National Public Radio, reported that Best Buy (among others) was identifying "devil shoppers" (that is, people who actively pursued bargains, repeatedly returned purchases to get better deals, and compulsively purchased only with coupons) as people who diverted selling resources from more valuable shoppers.[12] The bottom line of CRM is to invest in profitable customer relationships and turn away—or at least divert resources from—unprofitable customers.

Social networking can take CRM even further "by enriching critical sales practices with contextual information and relationship-building tools."[13] Shih suggests that *social networking* systems can be useful for establishing credibility, prospecting for new customers, gaining introductions, and providing references. She gives the example of Aster Data Systems:

> Aster Data Systems, a start-up software company in Silicon Valley, has dramatically grown its business through creative use of LinkedIn. . . . Senior management asked all employees, not just sales reps, to tap their networks for potential prospects that had . . . [specified] keywords in their title or functional expertise.[14]

Another opportunity to enhance business through CRM is "the promise of self-segmentation." Customers can be found in shared communities of interest. Such self-segmentation is "likely to be much more accurate and reflective of consumer's attributes than CRM data, since no one knows consumers . . . better than they know themselves."[15] This inexpensive, highly targeted access to customers has far-reaching implications for product development and customer service—and, therefore, operations management.

Social networks are just one kind of *social media*; they are more generally defined as Internet sites that allow users to create content and interact with other users. Other types of social media include content libraries (such as YouTube and Wikipedia), customer feedback and rating systems (like eBay and Amazon), and broadcast capabilities (such as Twitter). The growth rate of social media is astonishing; social networking site Facebook grew from 100 million to 200 million users in less than eight months; in March 2009, YouTube reached 100 million monthly viewers in the United States.[16] With trends like this, it would be foolhardy to overlook the potential business applications of social media.

Knowledge Management Systems

The last enterprise-wide system we will consider is also hard to implement and ripe with potential benefits. The *intellectual capital*, or knowledge, that is contained in an organization's collective can be very valuable if leveraged. In fact, intellectual capital is one of the few assets that gain value with use.

Knowledge can generally be considered value-added information held by individuals. The value comes from each person's judgment, experience, and context. Knowledge can be tacit, ingrained in the individual's contribution to the organization, or explicit, something that person knows he or she knows.

It has long been said that knowledge is power. This is especially true in today's competitive business environment, where intellectual capital can be the basis for a competitive advantage. If your company has someone who has knowledge in an area that someone else in the organization needs, a *knowledge management system* (*KMS*) can help the two people connect, whether they are two floors away or two continents apart. Business benefits can be winning more contracts, capitalizing on research ideas, or sharing cost-saving ideas.[17] This is extremely helpful in supporting operations in a wide range of industries, including consulting and professional services, and technology sales and support.

To implement a KMS requires organizational learning, where the organization captures what its employees know. Huber defined the contributing processes for organizational learning:[18]

- Knowledge acquisition, which includes capturing formal and informal learning, as well as making tacit knowledge explicit; scanning and possibly grafting new knowledge; and monitoring performance
- Information distribution, which means making knowledge accessible to the people who can use it

- Information interpretation, which involves providing context for the information and letting users know what to do with it
- Knowledge memorization to store and retrieve the information for later use

Like SCM systems, a KMS does not necessarily have to be computerized, but to leverage the intellectual capital across time and space, information technology must be used.

There are two key challenges that make it difficult to implement an effective KMS. Capturing the knowledge is time-consuming and often involves experts who do not want what they know to be captured. If you are valuable to your company because of your expertise in a specialized area, you want to protect your position. While the intellectual capital becomes more valuable if the company can leverage it, your personal capital is arguably diminished. Providing incentives such as recognition and rewards for experts, based on what is shared and how it is used, can mitigate this resistance.

The other challenge is the need for organizational unlearning. At what point do parts of the organizational memory become obsolete? Who determines this? By encouraging feedback on the contributions (think blog responses and customer ratings) and using meta-data (data about the data/ knowledge, such as the number of hits on a Web page or the click-through rate on banner advertisements), organizations can monitor the usefulness of a knowledge base.

Social media are taking KMS in new directions as well, with the creation of *knowledge networks*. As the focus of the firm shifts from internal control of knowledge to external collaboration, managers can create alliances where the distinction between organizations becomes blurred, and competitors, customers, and/or suppliers become partners as well.[19] One application of knowledge networks is peer production, "a way of producing goods and services that relies entirely on self-organizing, egalitarian communities of individuals who come together voluntarily to produce a shared outcome."[20] Internal reference systems for technology companies can be maintained easily with timely information using wikis. Beyond a single organization, Wikipedia is a fascinating example of peer production; open systems such as Linux system software development is another.

Producing goods and services puts social media at the heart of operations management, and some companies are learning to leverage peer production. It enables them to harness external talent, keep up with users, create demand for complimentary offerings, and reduce costs. Procter & Gamble has collaborated with organizations and individuals around the world, building on others' good ideas to bring new products such as Olay Regenerist and Swiffer Dusters to the consumer goods market.[21] In some cases, a manufacturer or producer has a problem that is looking for a solution in the knowledge network. In other cases, it might be that an innovator has a solution looking for a product application.

Future Directions

An emerging application of technology, with implications for collaboration across and beyond the organization, is *synthetic worlds*. Familiar to participants in Second Life and World of Warcraft games, synthetic worlds offer personalized graphical representations of users, known as *avatars*. Orlikowski describes a business application of a synthetic world created on an open source software infrastructure developed by Sun Microsystems. Called "Project Wonderland," the rooms, offices, screens, and documents are part of an online, three-dimensional, immersive environment for workplace collaboration. Participants' avatars are colocated with the underlying system and are manipulated using traditional devices (mouse, keyboard, microphone, and speakers) by the collaborators, who are geographically distant and might be suppliers, operations managers, customers, and internal or external experts. This software offers yet another extension of the enterprise-wide systems we have already discussed.[22] The use of avatars for communication, training, and collaboration is likely to become a common form of computer-mediated communications.

All of these enterprise-wide systems—SCM, ERP, CRM, and KMS—are complex, and the human factors to be considered are sizable. Training and developmental needs, job redesign and process changes, performance measurement, and incentive systems are affected by major systems implementations. Who owns the data? Who has access to data? Who can change information? These questions are even harder when using peer production.

As the systems become more complex, the human factors become even more important and harder to address. What happens to property rights with open source software? How much control should you impose on a knowledge network? Who monitors postings about your products and services in the blogosphere? How do you know that ratings and comments on products and services purchased over the Internet are made by real customers and not paid promoters?

For technology to be leveraged across and beyond an organization, it must first be put to use, or what is known as "into production." Installation may be as simple as loading software into storage devices connected to a server. Implementation, on the other hand, is when the technology is put to productive use. The extent to which a company can successfully implement such systems is based, in large part, on the maturity of its technology-related capabilities.

TECHNIQUE: CAPABILITY MATURITY MODELS

Sponsoring and participating in the implementation of an enterprise-wide system can be incredibly interesting—and dangerous. To avoid career-limiting moves, also known as "death-march" projects,[23] you want to have some way to evaluate your organization's likelihood of success, such as by using capability maturity models. This technique can also be useful in evaluating a prospective employer, if you ask the interviewer about the company's systems.

Another morbid characterization of the risk of large-scale technology implementations is the "suicide square." Implementation is a change in the existing situation, which can occur in any or all of three directions: new technology, new product, and new market. Change in any one of the dimensions represents risk; change in all three at once is considered suicide.[24]

For example, early in my career I was brought in on the recovery effort for the failed implementation of a new order-processing system, which was months behind schedule and far over its budget. Clearly in the suicide square, the project was supposed to use a new technology (a relational database management system) to offer a new product/application (online order processing) to a new market (group of users). Instead of trying to change everything at once, the company could have replaced an existing, familiar application with the new technology. Once they had experience with that technology, development team members would have been in a better position to create a new application. As it was, too many changes at once undermined the success of this project, and many careers suffered as a result.

Organizations may also lack the maturity to manage a systems development effort in a way that reduces implementation risks. *Maturity* implies a disciplined approach. It also reflects a consistency in capability.

A *capability maturity model* (*CMM*) is an evolutionary road map for implementing the vital practices from one or more domains of organizational process.[25] This means the model can be used as a guide over time (evolutionary road map) to reduce variability and improve quality (vital practices) for a wide range (one or more domains) of capabilities (organizational processes).

The more mature your organization is in a particular capability, the more successful it is likely to be in applying it.

The software maturity model is credited to Carnegie Mellon Software Engineering Institute (SEI), which developed it on behalf of the U.S. government. As the country was making greater and greater investments in information technologies, the government needed some way to evaluate a contractor's abilities, as well as the quality of its software development. With the enormous scale of the different systems used by the government and the strategic nature of some of the applications, software bugs could be catastrophic. The application of the maturity model framework has been extended from software development to people processes:[26]

> The People Capability Maturity Model (People CMM) is a framework that helps organizations successfully address their critical people issues. Based on the best current practices in fields such as human resources, knowledge management, and organizational development, the People CMM guides organizations in improving their processes for managing and developing their workforces. The People CMM helps organizations characterize the maturity of their workforce practices, establish a program of continuous workforce development, set priorities for improvement actions, integrate workforce development with process improvement, and establish a culture of excellence.

The original CMM has been retired and replaced by a more comprehensive framework that SEI refers to as *capability maturity model integration* (*CMMI*).

For our purposes, the original model with its broad applicability will suffice. The archetype maturity model has five levels of progression:

1. **Initial:** Also referred to as "chaotic," work is accomplished despite the organization; no apparent management systems are in place. New ventures and family-owned businesses that are closely held can often be found at this level.
2. **Managed:** There is some oversight of the work; expectations and processes are ill-defined or implicit. Academic institutions and professional services firms, where the "producers" are largely self-directed, tend to be at this level.
3. **Defined:** Processes are explicit; documentation of earlier work exists. This is probably the most common level, especially for medium and

large firms, because the work is less centrally controlled (and must therefore be documented).

4. **Predictable:** Variability is monitored; consistent results are demonstrated. Companies pursuing quality management usually fall into this category.

5. **Optimizing:** Provisions for continuous improvement exist; best practices are used. This is rare air, but it is the ultimate goal of a Six Sigma or lean approach to operations. Notice the parallels between the last two maturity indicators and the quality management principles described in Chapter 5. More mature organizations have consistent processes that are documented, monitored, and subject to continuous improvement.

A generalized hierarchy of maturity is presented in Figure 6-2, with the levels ranging from inconsistent to optimized.

While CMM and CMMI are proprietary to SEI, the general approach of the maturity model is not. Consulting organizations often use the idea as

Figure 6-2 General Maturity Model

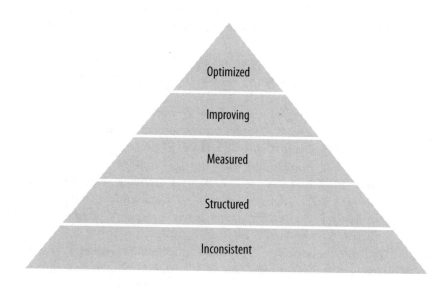

the basis for the methodology of their assessment services. For example, one consulting firm has applied a maturity model approach to corporate sustainability (that is, environmental responsibility) with the five levels represented as follows:[27]

1. Inactive/noncompliance
2. Basic compliance
3. Beyond compliance
4. Integrated sustainability
5. Sustainability leadership

In general, a capability maturity model is really a diagnostic tool. As you consider a prospective employer, whether or not to sign on for an enterprise-wide system project, or how to improve your operation's performance, you should evaluate the organization's maturity in key areas. What is done to ensure consistency? Is there a culture of continuous improvement? What performance metrics are used? How are problems handled? Is documentation of the capability in question readily available and current? Is the capability where you need it to be? Like any kind of organizational development, working on improving an organization's maturity costs money, needs executive support, and should have a specific strategic goal in mind.[28]

Application and Reflection
1. In the past week, in what way(s) did the use of technology help you overcome time and space barriers?
2. Where have you experienced the convergence of information and product or process technologies?
3. How can you stay current with technologies relevant to your field or industry?
4. In your own organization, how mature would you say your people processes are?

SUMMARY

As the physical manifestation of knowledge, technology can be used in products and processes, as well as in information systems. These types of technology are converging as information technology is used to enhance products and processes.

Technology is a mixed blessing; it can provide new opportunities by enabling organizations to transcend time and space, but these opportunities are available to both you and your competition.

While information technologies provide first-level effects, such as productivity or quality improvements, the more profound second-level effects result in social system changes. Information technology has enabled enterprise-wide systems, as well as interorganizational systems, to provide closer linkages, better coordination, and visibility across value chain. When technology is applied across the organization (through SCM, ERP, CRM, and KMS), the risk of implementation failure can be high because of the amount of complexity and change required. However, the potential benefits of such systems are compelling.

Social media offer new opportunities for content creation and collaboration. They can extend the capabilities of traditional enterprise systems for operations managers. For example, social networks can be used to gather customer requirements and monitor customer service; wikis can be used for knowledge networking within and beyond an organization's boundaries; and peer production can deliver new ideas for goods and services.

Maturity models are assessment tools to evaluate an organization's capability in a particular domain; more mature organizations have documented, consistent, and measured processes and a culture of continuous improvement that pursues best practices.

Review Questions

1. **Which of the following statements about technology is untrue?**
   a. It is the physical manifestation of knowledge.
   b. Process technology is defined as machines and material handling equipment.
   c. Technology can be knowledge manifest in products or processes.
   d. a and b
   e. b and c
2. **The Venn of technology illustrates the convergence of information technology with other types of technologies.**
   a. True
   b. False

3. It is important to capture as much information as possible about an operational process.
   a. True
   b. False

4. Which of the following is *not* a direct result of transcending time and space?
   a. Driving and enabling globalization
   b. Changing industry structures
   c. Creating access and immediacy
   d. a and b
   e. All of the above are direct results.

5. First-level effects of a technology are very difficult to quantify.
   a. True
   b. False

6. As technology changes the interrelationships between people and organizations, _____.
   a. they become more productive
   b. social system changes become evident
   c. human labor is replaced
   d. a and b
   e. All of the above

7. Information technology has the potential to do which of the following?
   a. Create unstructured processes
   b. Apply analytical methods to vast amounts of data
   c. Achieve quality management
   d. a and b
   e. All of the above

8. Which of the following enterprise-wide information systems is based on a definition of processes taken from best practices?
   a. SCM
   b. ERP
   c. CRM
   d. a and c
   e. All of the above

9. Social networking is a fad that should be ignored and restricted by businesses.
   a. True
   b. False

10. **Which of the following is *not* a characteristic of a maturity model?**
    a. It reflects a progression over time.
    b. The highest level of maturity results in an error-free environment.
    c. The more mature a capability is, the less variability it has.
    d. a and b
    e. All of the above are characteristic of maturity models.

PROCESS EFFECTIVENESS

If you can't describe what you are doing as a process,
you don't know what you're doing.
—W. EDWARDS DEMING

While it is important to have an organizational perspective of technology, quality, and effectiveness, most results are achieved through process and/or project management. This is the focus of our remaining chapters. First, we will examine ways to achieve organizational goals and competitive advantage through process effectiveness.

Recall that operational systems are transformational; they alter, store, inspect, and/or transport inputs into outputs by adding value. They can transcend organizational boundaries. And they can *always* be improved. Operational systems are a combination of processes. Some processes are an integral, or primary, part of the production function; others are not. In either case, process effectiveness is achieved in fundamentally the same ways.

After completing this chapter, you should be able to do the following:

- Design an effective new process
- Use a criteria-based evaluation to assess existing processes

- Identify potential pitfalls in *process change*
- Explain the *theory of constraints* and the importance of *throughput*
- Apply the five focusing steps for *process improvement*
- Prepare a process flow analysis

VALUE CHAIN PERSPECTIVE OF PROCESSES

In his definition of a *value chain*, Porter expanded our view of the transformation process and described operations as being composed of interdependent processes that transcend organizational boundaries.[1] It is in this chain of activities that value is added. The value chain perspective distinguishes between primary and secondary activities:

- **Primary activities:** inbound logistics, operations, outbound logistics, marketing and sales, and service
- **Secondary activities:** finance and administration, human resource management, and technological support

Primary activities directly contribute to the value of the goods and services provided by the operational system; *secondary activities* support the primary ones.

With this perspective, it is easy to see that operational systems can be classified as either production processes or business processes. Typically, the former are primary activities, and the latter are secondary ones. Remember that *production* describes the delivery of services as well as the manufacturing of goods. For our accounting friends, production processes contribute to direct costs, and business processes are part of the overhead.

To be clear on what constitutes a process, we will use Davenport and Short's definition of "logically related tasks performed to achieve a defined . . . outcome."[2] The logical relation implies a flow of goods as well as of information.[3] There is also a time element in the logic of a process as a chain of events.[4] For example, a bank's teller operation has a defined process for cash withdrawals. Presented with account information, typically on a withdrawal slip, the teller consults with an information system to verify the customer's identity and ensure that the necessary funds are available. Information is entered to record the transaction. The teller removes the requisite cash from the cash drawer. The money is counted out, in view of a camera, as it is given to the customer. The defined outcome of the process is a withdrawal. The logical relation is the flow of information to ensure that the funds are withdrawn from the current account, and the correct amount of cash is delivered. The sequence, or time element, of the process is important; the withdrawal slip must be presented first, as it would be foolhardy to give out cash without knowing who the customer was or how much cash was being requested.

Whether we are examining production processes or business processes, we can apply the principles of customer focus, teamwork, continuous improvement, value added, waste analysis, and managing for results to improve their effectiveness. A wide range of process effectiveness measures can be used. Efficiency (outputs/inputs) and capacity utilization have been traditional favorites. Although they are straightforward measures, they may not be the best indicators of effectiveness. For example, a company might be using all of its capacity but not satisfying its customers' demands, or it might be manufacturing to inventory without knowing if those finished goods will be sold. More enlightened operations managers (such as you) will look deeper for measures of effectiveness, as discussed in Chapter 3.

One of the most important measures of a process is its *throughput*, the rate at which inputs are converted into outputs. Whether you are evaluating an assembly line's cycle time or a restaurant's table turnover, you can evaluate how long it takes from the arrival of a customer request to its completion. Do you need to consider lead times for receiving materials? What about setup time? How does the need for flexibility affect the process throughput?

The other key measure of a process is its variability. We will cover this in depth in the next chapter. For now, suffice it to say that while some variability is inevitable, an effective process is highly consistent.

PROCESS DESIGN

The design of a process begins with the end, which means deciding what the process objectives are, typically in terms of end results and timing or throughput. As we saw with the new product development process in Chapter 4, the desired end result drives many other operational decisions, such as process form (project form, job shop, continuous flow, and so on), and there are trade-offs to be considered. For process design, basic trade-offs exist between capacity utilization, variability, and inventories, all of which are best decided on in the design phase.[5] The process objectives should also address the role of the customer in the process; the need for resource flexibility, including the level of automation; and whether the process will be performed in-house or outsourced (contracted out to a vendor).

For service firms, an additional decision must be addressed: where is the line of customer visibility? Beyond the extent of customers' involvement in the process, how much of the process should they see? *Decoupling* the "front-office" customer interface, which the customer can see, from the "back-office," unseen activities creates a division called the *line of visibility*. This decoupling is a common practice, although it is implemented in a variety of ways. Metters and Vargas identify what they call "potentially significant drawbacks" to decoupling:[6]

- The consistency of the service provided can be hindered by segregated duties; handoffs create waste in the process.
- Communications can be weaker between physically remote areas.
- Product or service flexibility can be hurt; for example, the ability to adapt to unique customer requests is diminished in a decoupled environment.

They suggest four different decoupling approaches:

- **Cost leader:** This method uses high decoupling to be a cost leader, as with GEICO insurance and Schwab investment services, where service is provided via the Internet or telephone, and staff are rarely face-to-face with customers.
- **Dedicated service:** This approach uses high decoupling in a high-cost environment to increase flexibility and support front-office personnel, as with real estate offices and their brokers or traditional hospitals establishing urgent care centers.
- **Cheap convenience:** This practice uses low decoupling and low cost to offer geographic dispersion, as with self-service kiosks.
- **Premium service:** This approach uses low decoupling and high cost to maximize customization and responsiveness, as with full-service spas and cruise ships.

The line of visibility is unique to each process, but in highly decoupled service processes, the customer has limited visibility. Charles Schwab customers may be assigned a financial advisor; although they exchange e-mails and speak over the telephone, the clients and advisor might never meet. To make this highly decoupled service seem more personal, the financial advisor's photograph appears on each client's personalized Schwab home page.

Conversely, when the process has high visibility and low decoupling, the customer is generally present and face-to-face with the service provider. On a Princess cruise ship, the service is highly personal and interactive. Yet much of the operation is unseen by customers, including laundry and kitchen operations, engineering and ship maintenance, and accounting. The line of visibility is quite apparent by the decor and the division of labor on board. Interestingly, some of the most popular excursions are the behind-the-scene tours of the ship.

Whether your production and businesses processes are tightly coupled or extremely decoupled, your process design should establish appropriate measurements for process performance. Measures should be taken at key points in the process as part of actionable feedback loops to ensure the quality of the operation and at bottlenecks to ensure that throughput is adequate. As we consider a number of criteria by which you can evaluate a process, it is important to remember that the hallmark of a quality system is to provide consistent results and obtain feedback useful for continuous improvement.

Criteria for Process Evaluation

We will assume that you now have an outline of a process, but is it a good process? Whether you are critiquing a new process design or analyzing an existing process, you should keep the guiding principles of customer focus, teamwork, continuous improvement, value, and waste analysis in mind. An appropriate criteria-based evaluation will ask the following questions:

- **Have we kept it simple?** Apply the Pareto principle to design for the routine (i.e., design for the 80 percent of the cases, rather than try to encompass every possible variation). Allow for exceptions, but do not overcomplicate the base process. The more complicated the process design, the more difficult the implementation, measurement, and continuous improvement will be—and the more likely it is to contain waste.
- **Is value added in each step?** Question whether support activities are really enabling primary ones. Activities that do not add value for the customer are opportunities for waste (see Chapter 5): overproduction, extra inventory, waiting, unnecessary transport, unnecessary processing, unnecessary human motions, and defects.

- **Have we minimized the handoffs?** Can the supplier/resource be changed to eliminate an extra part? Transitioning between people, machines, tools, and/or places adds time but not value to the process; however, not handing things off may place a greater burden on employees' skill sets or the costs of the resource. You must consider this trade-off in light of what is best for the customer. After all, if the customer is inconvenienced by a handoff or frustrated by an inadequately trained employee, the encounter will be unsatisfactory and could result in the loss of both a sale and a repeat customer.
- **Is each individual step and responsibility clearly defined?** When everyone knows what and how things are to be done, they are more likely to work as a team.
- **Have we included visual controls and/or fail-safe measures (poka yokes) for quality assurance?** Make it easy to be consistent.
- **Have we leveraged technology?** Determine whether technology can be used to add value, improve consistency, provide flexibility, or reduce costs. Consider whether the process could be paperless.
- **How do we monitor throughput and variability?** This will provide an early warning system for quality problems or process capacity issues. Process measurements can indicate opportunities for continuous improvement.

Whenever possible, you want to conduct a pilot test or a prototype of the process before attempting wide-scale implementation. This will allow you to refine the design and test your assumptions more easily. For example, are your measures reliable and meaningful? Can the process capacity handle the peak load? Are there sources of variability that can be eliminated? Issues like these are easier to address before the process is fully implemented. As we will discuss in the next section, changing an existing process is rife with challenges.

Changing Existing Processes

There's continuous improvement, and then there's serious change. Generally, it's easier to start fresh than to profoundly change something that already exists, especially if it's a firmly entrenched process. Process change tends to cause fear, uncertainty, and doubt in an organization: "Will I lose my job? Will I need new skills? How will I be evaluated? What if I lose clout?"

The need for significant process changes became a widespread phenomenon in the 1980s for two reasons. The first was the flurry of mergers and acquisitions, which meant the merging and/or acquiring new processes and often resulted in duplicated effort. The second was the advances in information technology, specifically enabling end-user computing and decision-support systems.

In their reengineering manifesto, Hammer and Champy provided guidelines for addressing processes needing significant overhaul:[7]

- Organize around outcomes, not tasks; for example, create an order processing department that does order entry and also handles order tracking and customer inquiries until the order is fully processed.
- Have those who use the output of the process perform the process; for instance, transfer some responsibility for self-service to the customer, as when an insurance company has a prospective customer enter information into an online quotation system.
- Subsume information-processing work into the real work that produces information; for example, have production line workers gather process control data in addition to their other duties.
- Treat geographically dispersed resources as though they were centralized; for instance, assemble project teams without regard to location.
- Place the decision point where the work is performed, and build control into the process; for example, allow line workers to stop a production line when a severe problem is detected.
- Capture information once and at the source (using source data automation); for instance, use bar codes for inventory or job handling.
- Don't automate, obliterate. If you automate an existing process that is ill-conceived, you will simply have a faster ill-conceived process.

This last admonition was deliberately startling when the authors first introduced the concept. The point was to get away from making incremental adjustments that tended to just add more steps to a process rather than streamline it. You might also note that obliterating will take you back to the first principles of process design.

Based on my own experiences with reengineering, I would add a few more suggestions. First, manage fear. Have empathy and be transparent. Peoples' jobs *will* change. Be clear about what the reengineering is intended to accomplish. And please do *not* use *reengineering* as a code word for "downsizing," or a reduction in force (RIF). It makes the rest of us who really do reengineering look bad.

Second, don't limit a solution by the personalities involved. You may have someone in the process who is just not going to be able to do the job that is required of him or her in the new process. Design it correctly anyway, and then work with the process owner to address the personnel problem. I have always been able to find such a person a new and acceptable role in such situations. In the same vein, you may have two people who do not want to work together. That should not constrain the process and should be dealt with separately as a personnel issue.

You should, however, consider job design in the context of the process design. As you consider what is to be done and how, take into account general human factors such as physical limitations and educational requirements. A common trade-off in job design is job specialization versus job expansion—a variation on the efficiency-flexibility trade-off. A more specialized worker is typically more efficient, although this can result in fatigue, injury, and/or errors when dealing with repetitive tasks. Expanding a job can be done by job enlargement, adding to the responsibilities; job enrichment, making it more interesting; and job rotations, providing temporary assignments. Job expansion requires more skill on the part of the worker, who may want higher compensation. However, a flexible workforce is more conducive to teamwork and better prepared for empowerment.

Last, and perhaps most important, have a high level of executive sponsorship. You will not win any popularity contests leading a reengineering project, and you may need the sponsor to do some metaphorical blocking and tackling for you to get the cooperation and support needed to get the job done. If the sponsor is only a midlevel manager and not at the executive level, you may be recommending him or her out of job to streamline a process.

Potential Pitfalls of Process Change

There are a lot of ways in which a reengineering effort can fail. When I use the term *failure*, I mean that the process does not change as needed. This may be a failure in design or a failure in implementation resulting from any or all of the following:[8]

- **An inability to reconceptualize processes.** It is better if the person leading the reengineering is not a part of the process, because it can be difficult for those involved to imagine any other way of doing things. Having an objective leader helps to avoid what is known as "paradigm paralysis." If you hear something like, "We've always done it this way," you know that's what you're facing.

- **Individualized work designs.** Design the process before you determine specific job assignments, or you may be creating unnecessary handoffs or designing around personalities.
- **Hierarchical decision making.** Middle managers rarely want to engineer themselves out of job, an approval process, or a budget center. Sponsors must have a broad view of the process and the need for its change.
- **Lack of recognition of benefits.** Establish a baseline before beginning any endeavor. Determine success metrics, so you can manage expectations.

On a more positive note, it *is* possible to implement change successfully. Briefly, the vision of the end result must be clear to everyone involved. That means it must be communicated often and in terms that everyone can understand (including what's in it for them, how their positions will be affected and measured, and so on). In the same way, people must understand the need for change and the consequences of not changing (such as loss of competitive position or a RIF). The difference between the vision and the consequence for not changing should be significant enough to create positive tension that motivates people to support the change. Highlighting successes as the change takes effect provides a valuable reinforcement and sustains the momentum of change.

ONGOING PROCESS MANAGEMENT

Ensuring process effectiveness on an ongoing basis requires measurements. However, you will find that performance measures are sometimes used for the wrong reasons. I believe some of this was caused by old-fashioned systems of cost accounting, where indirect costs were allocated by product, machine, or location. Some of it also arises from the justifications used for capital investments, where the return on investment is based on the number of widgets produced, so resource utilization is a focus. Another reason is that sometimes we use what is more easily measurable rather than what is meaningful.

Theory of Constraints

More than 20 years ago, Eliyahu Goldratt challenged that conventional thinking by writing a business novel that illustrated why a different perspective and measurement system made sense. *The Goal* not only created a new book genre, it greatly influenced management practice and has been published in numerous versions.[9] According to Sheinkopf, "The simple message of *The Goal* was: clarify the organization's purpose, determine measures that are aligned with that purpose, and improve by managing those few things that limit the organization's higher performance."[10]

So to start with, you have to know what the goal is. You may be surprised at what a hard question this can be. The answer is not about making products or delivering superior service or improving quality. Very simply, the goal is to make money now and in the future. Therefore, the focus of a process measurement system should be to (1) maximize throughput and (2) reduce operating costs, including waste, inventory, and so on.

Throughput determines the rate at which the process can achieve the goal. Therefore, understanding and addressing what is limiting, or constraining, a process's throughput is essential. This approach is known as the *theory of constraints* (*TOC*). To improve throughput, the "five steps of TOC" are broadly applicable to any process:[11]

1. Identify the constraint.
2. Decide how to exploit, or alleviate, the constraint.
3. Subordinate and synchronize everything else to the first two decisions.
4. Elevate (that is, improve) the performance of the constraint.
5. Determine the new constraint(s) and go back to step 1.

TOC thinking reinforces many of the quality practices we examined in Chapter 5, although the terminology is slightly different.

We typically think of constraints as bottlenecks, resources whose capacity is less than demand. A bottleneck can be physical, such as a machine that cannot reliably go any faster. It can also be a person, perhaps a cook who cannot keep pace with the number of orders coming into the kitchen or a manager who lets approvals sit on his or her desk for days.

Exploiting a constraint may involve changing a policy or employing a new paradigm (such as a new method or technology).[12] Very often, it means finding a way to leverage existing capacity. In the short term, this may entail managing demand by increasing prices to limit the volume or offering promotions to change the timing. On the supply side, increasing operating hours in manufacturing is a quick fix.

An interesting example is provided by a French supermarket chain, Chronodrive. To increase sales by offering customers greater convenience over traditional supermarket shopping, Chronodrive offers online ordering and drive-through pickup for groceries. According to *The Wall Street Journal*, "Customers order online—or can even use a terminal outside the store to make quick orders for any of the 500 products it makes immediately available. When ordering online you can choose your time for pickup; orders can be ready in two hours after purchase online, and delivery to your car trunk by Chronodrive's workers is guaranteed within five minutes of pulling up to the warehouse." The chain's management identified that throughput was constrained by the steps needed to remove items from freezer units. To elevate this constraint, Chronodrive has replaced freezer units with freezer rooms, making it possible for staff to fill orders more quickly.[13]

Capacity Management

Goldratt advocates a systems view of capacity, by which you balance the flow and not the capacity. This is where subordination comes into play. You are probably familiar with the concept of balanced performance from using a computer. You may have a fast processor and scads of disk space, but if you don't have enough memory, the system will be slowed by that one constraint. In manufacturing, this is known as *synchronous manufacturing*, meaning the entire process is working together in harmony; the emphasis is on system performance, not localized measures. Everything is subordinate to the bottleneck.

Of course, this harmony is idealized; in reality, there will be variations. When fluctuations occur in a dependent sequence (process) without any inventory between workstations and one step takes longer than the average, there is no opportunity to make up that time in the subsequent steps. This would imply that it is better to have more capacity earlier in the process, so less overall time is lost. It also implies that you should "never starve a bottleneck," letting constraining resources go idle. This may require some work in process inventory ahead of the bottleneck. It's a trade-off.

Scheduling can also be used as a capacity lever to elevate a constraint, but it is often not an easy solution. Scheduling related to the timing of the use of resources means ensuring that the *right* tasks are conducted at the *right* time on the *right* items. Throughput or productivity problems are often attributable to poor schedule management and demand variability. Cellular phone discounts for calls in the evenings and on weekends is an attempt to shift the timing of the demand to time periods when more capacity is unused.

The amount of insight you have into demand patterns will have a significant impact on your ability to match scheduling to demand. This can be particularly difficult for job shop processes, where the sequence of operations varies. Technologies such as enterprise resource planning systems have much to offer in this area, including bills of materials, interactive scheduling, and order visibility.

Capacity cushions, resource flexibility, inventory, and longer lead times also serve as ways to elevate constraints and provide buffers against uncertainty; however, costs are associated with all of them and can hide systemic issues. (Remember the JIT metaphor of the boat cruising above the rocks in Chapter 5?) Computer simulations, mathematical models, and scheduling software can be useful tools in predicting demand and allocating resources. The state of the art in these technologies changes regularly and is therefore beyond the scope of this book, so the following tips will suffice for our purpose:

- Having good historical data will make the tools more useful.
- Performing sensitivity analysis—evaluating how decisions or schedules might change, given changes in assumptions—is a valuable part of any of these tools. One of the most important questions an operations manager can ask is, "What if?"
- Evaluating software options can be seductive. Don't be swayed by features you are unlikely to use. It is better to have a tool you can wield effectively than a more complex tool that you have to relearn every time you use it. Look for tools that are not only easy to use, but easy to learn *and* easy to remember.

Training and experience can also complicate scheduling by adding to the variability of resources. An interesting concept to consider is the learning curve. A commonsense interpretation tells you that the more often someone performs a task, the less time it will take him or her—up to a point. Mathematically, the learning curve function originated in the airframe manufacturing industry. It was observed that each time output doubled, labor hour per plane decreased by a fixed percentage. This was represented by the logarithmic function, $M = mN^r$, where M = labor hours for Nth unit, m = labor hours for first unit, N = number of units produced, and r = exponent of curve (or log[learning rate]/0.693). The mathematics has not been as generally applicable as the concept of a learning curve has been.

The bottom line is that the effectiveness of a process comes from its design (or redesign), effective measurements, and feedback loops. Peak performance comes from managing throughput by addressing constraints, capacity uses, and resource scheduling. One way to gain a grasp on what is happening in a process is to use a visual technique known as flowcharting. Flowcharts can be useful for process description as well as analysis.

TECHNIQUE: FLOWCHARTING

Since I aspire to grow old without becoming cynical, I will simply say that every consulting company and most technical disciplines have their own way of charting the flow of a process. Let me offer a commonsense approach by starting with why we would want to flowchart and what information we want to show. (We can argue about symbols and colors later!)

We create a flowchart to improve our understanding of a process. It may be a training tool for a new employee, a guide to ensure consistency in following the process steps, or a sales tool to help prospective clients understand the service a vendor is offering. Perhaps most importantly, we use flowcharts to identify measurement needs and possible improvements.

With these varied uses in mind, what should the chart contain?

- Starting and stopping points
- Individual steps and decision points
- Sequences of steps and points

Sometimes all we see in a flowchart are boxes containing points and steps, with arrows indicating sequences. Many layers of meaning can be added to enhance the chart's usefulness; here are a few:

- Time elements for each step, including any delays
- Types of actions in each step (such as alter, inspect, transport, and store)
- Physical locations for each step and distances for any transport
- Resources (including the customer) used for each step
- Material and information flows in and out of each step

This information can be embedded in the chart as text; represented by using shapes, colors, and relative position; and coded with symbols. Information designer Stephen Few describes the use of visual attributes that we are able to perceive intuitively in a quantitative manner, including length, width, orientation, size, shape, curvature, enclosure, spatial grouping, blur, hue, and color intensity.[14] For example, the matrix in Table 7-1 shows some of the possible ways to provide additional layers of meaning, or cues, in a flowchart.

Table 7-1   Sources of Meaning in Flowcharts

Element	Cue	Options
Time elements for each step, including any delays	Use the relative position of the steps to indicate a progression of time from left to right.	Embed the time in the process step description; also create "steps" for delays.
Types of actions in each step (such as alter, inspect, transport, and store)	Use the shape of the "box" indicating the step to show the type of action or a delay.	It does not matter what shape you use, as long as you are explicit in your legend about what the shape means.
Physical locations for each step and distances for any transport	Position is also useful here; think of the flowchart as having rows that represent different departments or locations.	Note travel distances as labels on the arrows that indicate the sequence of the steps. For services, you will want to note the line of customer visibility, usually treated as a dotted line across the page.
Resources (including the customer) used for each step	Color (or border pattern, if you're limited to black and white) is a good way to distinguish who is involved.	This may not be necessary if resource and location represent essentially the same information.
Material and information flows in and out of each step	Use text on the arrows (materials on top, information underneath) or footnotes to indicate flows.	If the chart gets too cluttered, you can create a separate data flow diagram.

Because of my background in industrial engineering and information technology, I tend to use an amalgam of conventions from both fields: alter = rectangle; transport = fat arrow; store = square; inspect = triangle; delay = semicircle; decision = diamond; starts/stops = circles.

The most important element is that you have a legend that makes these cues specific. Keep the purpose of the flowchart in mind. If you are redesigning an existing process, the chart should inform the need for improvements. Information flows might be crucial for a systems development project but superfluous for training purposes.

Let's look at a typical example. Figure 7-1 shows a manufacturing process for bakery bread production. This type of flowchart has many good features. The sequence of steps is clear. Presented in a tabular format, each step has information about what it is, how long it takes, and how far it goes. A quick glance at the symbols indicates delays that may be eliminated or coincide with other steps, i.e., have the worker do something productive while waiting, if the delay is inevitable. Distance traveled and time taken for each step are noted and totaled in the top left corner. In a

Figure 7-1   Excerpt of Flow Chart Example

Summary	No.	Min.	Operation: Bakery Bread Production
○ Alter	10	68.00	Charted by: Ima Baker
→ Transport	3	11.00	Present Method
△ Store	3	2.00	
D Delay	3	160.00	
□ Inspect	2	9.00	
Total	**21**	**250.00**	
Feet of Travel	**90**		

No.	Dist (ft.)	Time (min.)	Alter	Transport	Store	Delay	Inspect	Description
1	20	5	○	➡	△	D	□	Gather ingredients from storage
2		0.5	●	→	△	D	□	Mix yeast and water
3		15	○	→	△	D	□	Let yeast soak
4		2	●	→	△	D	□	Sift flour
5		4	○	→	△	D	■	Measure ingredients

lean production, you might want to explore the possibility of keeping the supplies nearby to reduce travel back and forth from inventory. You might also wonder if the 160 minutes of delay time might be shortened with faster-acting yeast.

A typical services chart is presented in Figure 7-2. Here, the layout makes it a little difficult to follow the process, and the line of visibility to the customer is confusing. Is the customer to the left of the line or to the right? Aren't customers able to see the streetlight being repaired? With services, you want to scrutinize customers' involvement in the process. You should ensure that the amount of visibility to the customer is intentional and appropriate. It is also advisable to consider how customers' time is used. In this case, you would want to know why the customer has to call the company to be referred to the website. Perhaps that information could be printed on the bill with the telephone number.

When developing your own flowcharts, think about how you want to use each one. Are you adding enough information to use our criteria for process evaluation? Does the chart show whether the process does the following:

- Keeps it simple
- Adds value at each step
- Minimizes handoffs
- Clearly defines each individual step and responsibility
- Includes quality assurance
- Leverages technology
- Monitors throughput and variability

Consider the different sources of waste and delays that may be evident. Are there safety concerns? Make sure you understand where the process begins and ends, and identify interdependencies with other processes. Let the flowchart tell it all.

Application and Reflection

1. Think of a recent situation in which you have been a victim of poor throughput. What do you think caused the problem?
2. Give an example of where you have experienced or observed a learning curve.

Figure 7-2   Services Flow: Repair Service

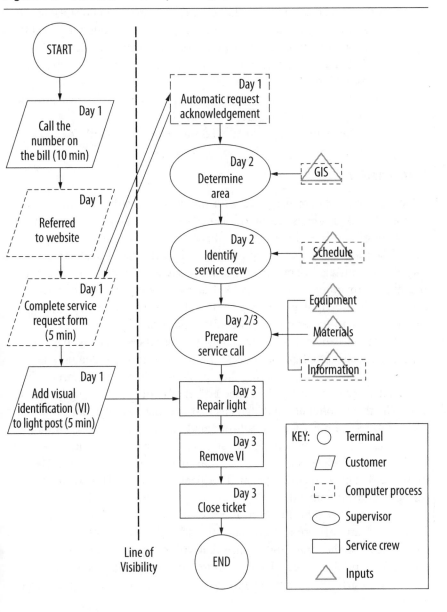

3. Find a simple process to evaluate—either as a customer, an observer, or a performer. Describe the process in terms of end results and timing or throughput: see if you can determine the following, and then evaluate the process against our criteria for process design.
   a. What is the process form (project form, job shop, continuous flow)?
   b. What is the extent of customer involvement (physical presence, personal attention, method of delivery)?
   c. Where might there be a need for resource flexibility?

SUMMARY

Effective processes are designed with the desired results in mind, and the design addresses process form and capacity requirements, resource needs, the extent of customer involvement, variability sources, and interdependencies. When assessing existing processes, a criteria-based evaluation should consider simplification, opportunities for waste elimination, visual controls, and excess inventory. Is value added at every step? If not, can steps be eliminated? Is technology leveraged cost-effectively? Are there appropriate measurements to monitor process quality and throughput?

Processes can be difficult to change because the people involved may be unable to reconceptualize the process, be invested in individual job designs, or limit possibilities by protecting their positions. Fear is an important factor to consider. Be clear about the expected benefits of changing the process.

The theory of constraints tells us that in order to make money now and in the future, we must focus on throughput and cost reduction. Throughput determines the rate at which the operation can make money, so it is important to identify and address constraints. Note that as one constraint is elevated (improved), a new one may appear. The ideal is balanced flow with adequate capacity to meet demand.

Process flowcharts help to improve our understanding of a process. There are many different approaches to and styles of flowcharts. Focus on the purpose of the chart and ensure that you have the necessary information. Use symbols, colors, shapes, and textures to add layers of meaning to the text and arrows; be sure to include a legend that explains the purpose of each.

Review Questions

1. Which of the following is *not* a characteristic of an effective new process?
   a. Primary activities add value.
   b. Throughput is a key performance measure.
   c. Capacity utilization is a crucial indicator.
   d. Loops in the process provide feedback about quality.
2. Highly decoupled services have no line of visibility, since the customer cannot see much of the operation.
   a. True
   b. False
3. Which of the following is *not* a criterion for evaluating process effectiveness?
   a. Documentation
   b. Clarity
   c. Simplicity
   d. Consistency
4. What makes reengineering existing processes so difficult?
   a. Organizing around outcomes is counterintuitive.
   b. Obliterating is fun, so everyone wants to do it.
   c. Decision points become geographically dispersed.
   d. Employees worry about job changes and eliminations.
5. It is advisable to establish baseline measures of performance before changing a process.
   a. True
   b. False
6. It is easier to reconceptualize a process when you work with it.
   a. True
   b. False
7. Why is throughput important?
   a. It indicates how quickly you are making money.
   b. It indicates how high equipment utilizations are.
   c. It clarifies the organization's purpose.
   d. It determines how to allocate overhead costs.
8. Which of the following statements about the theory of constraints is *not* true?
   a. The goal is to make money now and in the future.
   b. Operating costs should not be a consideration; only throughput matters.
   c. Inventory may be appropriate before a bottleneck.
   d. Time lost in a dependent sequence cannot be regained.

9. **Place the five focusing steps in the correct order:**
   a. Elevate the performance of the constraint.
   b. Subordinate and synchronize the process to the rate of bottleneck production.
   c. Decide how to exploit the constraint.
   d. Identify the constraint.
   e. Determine the new constraints and repeat.

10. **Process flowcharts can use which of the following attributes to convey meaning?**
    a. Length and width
    b. Color and patterns
    c. Shapes
    d. b and c
    e. All of the above can be used.

8

PROCESS QUALITY

Assignable causes of variation may be found
and eliminated.

—WALTER A. SHEWHART

I n the last chapter, we learned how to design new processes, analyze existing processes, implement reengineered processes, and manage throughput. But once you have a good process in place, how do you keep it running smoothly? How will you know if it's "under control"?

In the arena of process quality, *control* has a very specific meaning and is defined in statistical terms. Don't panic if you're mathphobic. Conceptually, a process is under control if the quality measures taken are not improbable. In other words, your process is out of control if you take samples and get results that would be highly unlikely to occur if it were *in* control.

As we examine the topic of process quality in more detail, we will start with a refresher on some statistical concepts. After that review, you will be ready to look into what and how you take measurements and determine the limits of control for a process. Then we will put all of this information in context, so you understand how to interpret what you have measured.

After completing this chapter, you should be able to do the following:

- Distinguish between common and assignable causes of variation
- Understand the theoretical foundation for *statistical process control*
- Identify implementation considerations for statistical process control
- Create and interpret statistical process *control charts*
- Evaluate a process's *capability* to meet specifications

THEORETICAL FOUNDATION

For our refresher in statistical concepts, we start first with the elegant simplicity of normal distribution. I could wax poetic about normal distribution:

The curve is impressive, so smooth and symmetrical
The way it predicts so many things is magical.
All we really need to know is how tall and how wide
To use it for processes, just turn it on its side.

All kidding aside, we really are fortunate that the *normal distribution* is at the heart of statistical process control (SPC). Every part of the continuous curve can be determined by just two parameters—the mean and the standard deviation. (Yes, the calculations of the probability densities were made according to a complicated function, but someone has already done those calculations and tabulated them, so we don't need to worry about them!)

Characteristics of the Normal Distribution

Any variable that we describe as "normally distributed" follows the same pattern. The *mean* determines how "tall" the curve gets, and the *standard deviation* tells us how spread out it is. Then, no matter what normally distributed variable we are evaluating, we always know that one standard deviation (or 1σ) above and below the mean represents 68 percent of all the possible values for the variable. Plus or minus two standard deviations (2σ) is 95 percent, and plus or minus three (3σ) covers 99.7 percent of the possibilities, as shown in Figure 8-1. It doesn't matter what the mean or the standard deviation is, this probability density function will *always* be the same.

This is true whether you are comparing human characteristics, such as men's heights and standardized test results, or measuring other phenomena such as laser light density. Better yet, the normal distribution is often used to

Figure 8-1 Normal Distribution

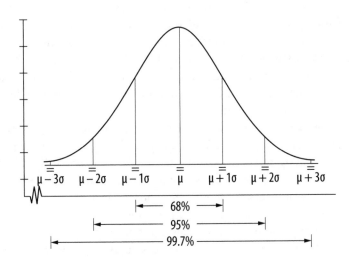

approximate other types of distributions, because of the applicability of the *central limit theorem* (CLT).* Best of all, we can use the normal distribution to determine if a process is out of control by taking samples, calculating sample statistics, and plotting them in chronological order. If the distribution of the sample statistics does not change over time, the process is considered to be in a state of statistical control.[1]

Common Versus Assignable Causes of Variability

We want to know if a process is out of control so we will know when we need to make adjustments. All processes have variability. Think about styling your hair on a steamy July day in Georgia and then on a chilly November day in Denver. Same hair. Same hair care products. Same comb and brush.

---

*According to Pierre-Simon LaPlace, the central limit theorem states, "Consider a random sample of n observations selected from a population (*any* probability distribution) with mean μ and standard deviation $\sigma_{X\text{-bar}} = \sigma/\sqrt{n}$. The larger the sample size, the better will be the normal approximation to the sampling distribution of $\overline{X}$ (sample mean)."

In this case, it is environmental factors like humidity level, temperature, and altitude that create the variability.

As we know, *variability* is undesirable and costly, so we want to have as little of it as possible. It is unrealistic, though, to measure every aspect of a process and then make adjustments after each measurement. Process adjustments are costly because they slow throughput and consume resources (such as the time of the people making the adjustments). Measurements are costly because they take time. So we want to be judicious in deciding what we measure and when we adjust.

Common causes, also known as natural causes, are the purely random, unidentifiable sources of variation that are unavoidable in a specific process. In addition to environmental factors, there may be machine limitations or vibrations, as well as human factors that are inherent in the process. A process is "robust" if it is less susceptible to common causes of variation. Over the long term, you may be able to reduce this amount of variability with fundamental changes to the process (new equipment, materials, technologies, and so on). In the short term, however, process adjustments are *not* warranted for common causes (and can actually make the variability worse).

Assignable causes (sometimes referred to as special causes) include any factors that can be identified and eliminated, as stated in the opening quotation from the father of statistical process control, Walter A. Shewhart. Tool wear, training concerns, and raw material issues are all examples of assignable causes. The six major sources of process variation are (1) people, (2) machines, (3) materials, (4) methods, (5) measurement, and (6) environment.[2] The variations may be in terms of spread (the dispersion of the measurements) or amount (the central tendency).

This is illustrated in Figure 8-2. You can see in the first schematic that the two distributions are the same in width and height but are centered on different points, indicating a shift in central tendency (the mean). In the second schematic, the two distributions are centered at the same mean, but the height and width of the normal curves vary because of differences in variation (the standard deviation).

When assignable causes are present, process adjustment may be warranted. The action to be taken is situation-dependent, considering the cost of adjustment and the risk of poor quality. In some cases, a production line will be stopped immediately to investigate and ensure that no further assignable variation occurs. In other cases, the action might simply be to take more measurements and then decide what to do.

Figure 8-2   Changes in Normal Distributions

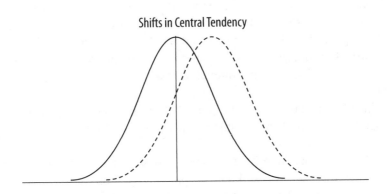

Shifts in Central Tendency

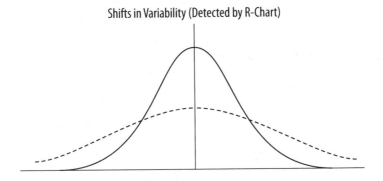

Shifts in Variability (Detected by R-Chart)

You might ask, "How can I tell if assignable causes are present?" The answer is that the normal distribution tells you. First you establish what variability you expect under normal circumstances (pun intended) and create a process control chart. Then if you take a sample and the sample's statistics are improbable (according to all you know about the normal distribution), then you likely have an assignable cause. The following section explains how to create control charts and interpret them to determine whether assignable causes are present.

CONTROL CHARTS

To understand how assignable causes are identified, it is helpful to understand what a process control chart looks like. An example is shown in Figure 8-3. Look at it as turning the normal distribution on its side to create the *y*-axis; the *x*-axis is simply time. The dashed lines indicate standard deviation intervals above and below the mean, with the center line representing the mean of the distribution. Samples are taken and plotted in chronological order.

To identify an improbable point based on what we know about the normal distribution, there are some simple rules of thumb:[3]

- One point outside of three standard deviations on either side of the center line (because we know the probability of this is 100 percent–99.7 percent, or 0.003, three chances in a thousand). These limits are designated as the upper control limit (UCL) and lower control limit (LCL) in Figure 8-3.

Figure 8-3   Sample Control Chart

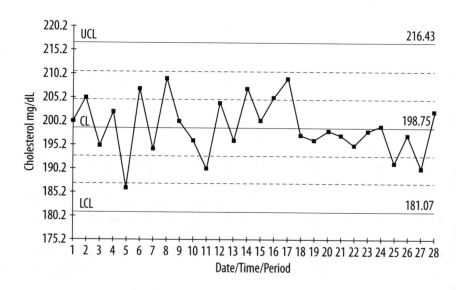

- Two successive points between the second and third deviation on the same side of the center line (this is half the difference between 99.7 percent and 95.5 percent, squared, or 0.0004).
- Seven successive points that are all above or below the mean (each one has a probability of 50 percent; taken successively, the probability of seven occurring in a row is 0.5^7, which is about 0.007).

Another thing to keep in mind is the "rule of five," which says that five successively increasing (or decreasing) points looks like a trend and signals a process shift. There are many variations to these rules, all of which are intended to identify improbable occurrences, but some of which have complex underlying calculations.

Attributes Versus Variables

A wide variety of control charts are used, and their appropriateness is based on what is being measured and the calculated statistics. One way to determine what chart type to use is to consider whether you are using qualitative or quantitative data. This can be a little confusing at first, because in both cases you are using numbers.

Numerical values of qualitative data are things like number of defects (count) or fraction defective (percentage). They are used when you measure attributes, quality characteristics that have discrete values, such as defective versus not defective. In these cases, you generally use attribute charts such as c-charts (based on the count of flaws in a sample) or p-charts (based on the percentage of defective items in a sample).

Quantitative data are tracked as variables, measures that are continuous and use rational numbers. Rational numbers are those for which ratios are valid (for example, a 4.4-foot board is 2:1 longer than a 2.2-foot board). Examples are thickness, length, weight, and so on. When you are controlling by (or for) variables, you must use both charts. Why? Refer back to Figure 8-2. You need the $\overline{X}$ chart to determine if there has been a shift in central tendency; the R-chart alerts you to changes in the spread. Ranges are used in lieu of standard deviations to measure the spread, as an approximation that is much easier to calculate when collecting the data.

Chart Mechanics

How best to get started with statistical process control seems like the chicken-and-egg conundrum—which came first? How can you construct a control chart if you don't know whether your process is under control?

Ideally, the center line and control limits should be developed using data that were collected during a period when you believe the process was in control. Technically, though, you cannot determine whether the process is in control until after you have constructed a control chart. So, practically speaking, when a control chart is first constructed, the center line and control limits are treated as temporary limits or trial values.[4]

In my experience, you start with 30 or more samples, calculate the sample statistics that you are charting, establish the control limits based on those statistics, and then plot the values of the statistics. If you do not detect any statistical improbabilities in these 30 points, you may consider the limits usable. If you do find that some part of the sample violates our rules of thumb, you should investigate for special causes, correct them, and then measure again.

When developing a control chart, you have three decisions to make. First, what quality characteristic of interest do you want to measure? Second, what is your sampling plan? Third, how much error are you willing to risk in your control evaluation?

The quality characteristic you will measure is an important choice, because measuring output has associated costs—the time to measure, chart, and analyze, and in some cases, the cost of waste if the product cannot be used after the sample is taken. So measurements should be taken where the cost of poor quality is the greatest:

- Before a bottleneck (because you do not want to waste bottleneck resources processing things that are of low quality)
- Before a step that would obscure important quality characteristics (for example, once you seal a box or paint on the finish, it might be hard to detect underlying flaws)
- Before an expensive or hard-to-correct process is performed (for reasons similar to those with the bottleneck)

The sampling plan should be designed to ensure randomness (at different times every day, during different shifts, and so on) to maximize the potential for between-sample variability. The samples should be small to minimize the variability within the sample (otherwise, wild fluctuations with extreme values will offset one another).

The number examined (or collected) should be the same for every sample. Typically, the sample size (n) is small, meaning less than 10. It has to be logical or rational for your process. If you are inspecting hotel rooms that the housekeeping staff have cleaned and you have five maids in the crew, you would inspect a room done by each one at random intervals, so the sample size would be 5. If you are evaluating the output of a machine that has four sets of 10 nozzles, your best sample would be from one nozzle in each of the four sets ($n = 4$), at various times during the day.

Finally, the risk of error comes from determining how many standard deviations you want to include in your chart. If you set your control limits at $\pm 3\sigma$, your risk of being wrong (thinking the process is out of control when it is not) is $100\% - 99.7\% = 0.3\%$. As you apply the additional rules of thumb (which assume $\pm 3\sigma$ limits), the probability of being wrong is further reduced. In this chapter, we will use $\pm 3\sigma$ limits in the examples, which is typical.

With these decisions made, the construction of the control chart is quite simple:

1. Take 30 or more (N) samples of size n.
2. Calculate the sample statistic(s) to be used in the control chart.
3. Set the center line at the mean of the N samples' statistics.
4. Estimate the standard deviation (σ) of the process (How you estimate σ will vary, depending on which chart you use, as shown in Table 8-1.)

Table 8-1   Control Chart Calculations

Chart	Center Line	UCL	LCL
$\bar{X}$	$\bar{\bar{X}}$	$\bar{\bar{X}} + A_2 {}^*\bar{R}$	$\bar{\bar{X}} - A_2 {}^*\bar{R}$
R	$\bar{R}$	$D_4 {}^*\bar{R}$	$D_3 {}^*\bar{R}$
c	$\bar{c}$	$\bar{c} + 3 {}^*\sqrt{\bar{c}}$	$\bar{c} - 3 {}^*\sqrt{\bar{c}}$
p	$\bar{p}$	$\bar{p} + 3 {}^*\sqrt{[\bar{p}(1 - \bar{p})/n]}$	$\bar{p} - 3 {}^*\sqrt{[\bar{p}(1 - \bar{p})/n]}$

5. Set the upper control limit and lower control limit at $\pm 3\sigma$ (estimated), respectively.

6. Plot the samples' statistics on the chart in chronological order.

Note that in step 4, we estimate the standard deviation of the samples rather than calculate it directly. This is because we can invoke the use of the normal distribution, so the factors for the estimation are tabulated. Examine Table 8-1. The top half shows the formulas and factors used in calculating the control limits for our four main types of charts. Note that $\overline{X}$ is the sample mean; $\overline{\overline{X}}$ is the mean of the sample means (the "grand mean"); $\overline{R}$ is the mean of the sample ranges; $\overline{c}$ is the mean of the sample counts; and $\overline{p}$ is the mean of the sample defective proportions.

For control charts by variables, the factors A_2, D_3, and D_4 are based on the sample size and are tabulated in Table 8-2. These factors are multipliers that allow us to use the range (R) to approximate the standard deviation of the process. This makes for quicker calculations, especially when you have a production worker updating the chart on the production floor.

For control charts by attributes, we typically work with counts or fraction defective. While counts (c) are Poisson-distributed and fraction defective (p) follows a binomial distribution, we can invoke the CLT and use the normal distribution to estimate the mean and the standard deviation of both distributions. Both statistics can be calculated by knowing only the average percent defective or the average count. That makes it easy to develop either

Table 8-2 Tabulated Factors for Control Chart Calculations

n	Factor A_2	Factor D_4	Factor D_3
2	1.88	0.00	3.27
3	1.02	0.00	2.57
4	0.73	0.00	2.28
5	0.58	0.00	2.11
7	0.42	0.08	1.92
10	0.31	0.22	1.78
20	0.18	0.41	1.59

a *p*- or *c*-chart. When controlling by attributes, we only need to consider one chart to look for assignable causes.

Statistical Process Control Illustrations

Suppose you are responsible for an operation that cans beans. The cans are labeled "Net weight 14 ounces." Indeed, an overall process average of 16 ounces has been found by taking many samples, in which each sample contained 5 cans. The average range of the process has been 0.25 ounces.

From this narrative, we know that $\overline{X} = 16.0$; $\overline{R} = 0.25$; and $n = 5.0$. Consulting the table of factors for $n = 5$, we find that $A_2 = 0.58$, $D_4 = 0.00$, and $D_3 = 2.11$. With a center line of 12, the control limits for the $\overline{X}$ chart are as follows:

$$UCL\overline{X} = 16 + (0.58 \times 0.25) = 16.14 \text{ ounces}$$
$$LCL\overline{X} = 16 - (0.58 \times 0.25) = 15.86 \text{ ounces}$$

Accordingly, here are the control limits for the R-chart:

$$UCL_R = 0.25 \times 0 = 0$$
$$LCL_R = 0.25 \times 2.11 = 0.53$$

with a center line of 0.25. Note in this example that the R-chart is not symmetrical. That is because negative values of a range are impossible, so the normal distribution is truncated at R = 0. Half of the probability density is still below the center line, although it would look skewed if you drew it.

To look at another illustration where the normal distribution is truncated at 0, we will use an example of control by attributes. Say you are the owner of a landscaping company. You send out multiple crews each day to mow, edge, and blow clippings for your clients' yards. Since you cannot directly supervise each crew, you have implemented a random sampling approach to evaluate the quality of service your company provides. When you inspect a job, there are a number of possible defects, such as an unmowed patch of grass (also known as a "mohawk"); sloppy edging along the walkways; and residual clippings left in the street. Of course, each yard can have multiple defects. Over the past two years, you have determined that the average is 2.4 so the UCL for the *c*-chart is 7 and the LCL for the *c*-chart is 0. In the

Figure 8-4a   Sample of Statistical Control Chart

LCL	$\bar{c}$	$\bar{c}+1*\sqrt{\bar{c}}$	$\bar{c}+2*\sqrt{\bar{c}}$	UCL	c_i
0	2.4	3.9	5.5	7.1	3
0	2.4	3.9	5.5	7.1	1
0	2.4	3.9	5.5	7.1	3
0	2.4	3.9	5.5	7.1	1
0	2.4	3.9	5.5	7.1	0
0	2.4	3.9	5.5	7.1	2
0	2.4	3.9	5.5	7.1	5
0	2.4	3.9	5.5	7.1	0
0	2.4	3.9	5.5	7.1	4
0	2.4	3.9	5.5	7.1	2
0	2.4	3.9	5.5	7.1	4
0	2.4	3.9	5.5	7.1	1
0	2.4	3.9	5.5	7.1	0
0	2.4	3.9	5.5	7.1	0
0	2.4	3.9	5.5	7.1	2
0	2.4	3.9	5.5	7.1	3
0	2.4	3.9	5.5	7.1	6
0	2.4	3.9	5.5	7.1	5
0	2.4	3.9	5.5	7.1	4
0	2.4	3.9	5.5	7.1	5
0	2.4	3.9	5.5	7.1	4

past month, you have inspected 23 jobs and calculated and plotted the results presented in Figure 8-4a and 8-4b.

At first glance, the interpretation of this control chart may be confusing, because the center line is not halfway between the UCL and the LCL. To clarify, lines have been added to represent one and two standard deviations above the mean (the $\bar{c}$). Three standard deviations above the mean is the UCL. Examining the chart for an improbable point, you apply our rules of thumb:

- Is there one point outside of three standard deviations on either side of the center line? No.
- Are there two successive points between the second ($c = 5.5$) and third deviation ($c = 7.1$) above the center line? No. However, if you look

Figure 8-4b   Sample of C-Chart

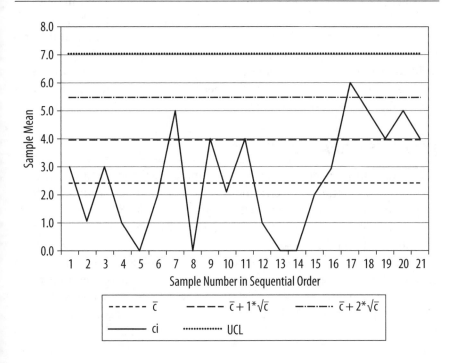

below the center line, you see two counts of 0 in a row. That is not really improbable, because two standard deviations below the center line would be 2.4–3.1, so there is more probability density below 0 than just the difference between the second and third deviation. Practically speaking, having two samples in a row with no defects is a good thing anyway.

- Are there five successively increasing (or decreasing) points in a row? No.
- Are there seven successive points that are all above or below the mean? No, but if the next sample has three or more defects, that would indicate there is probably a shift (a higher number of defects per sample than you would expect with $\bar{c} = 2.4$), since the previous six points are above the mean (3, 6, 5, 4, 5, 4).

Another point to consider when using a *c*-chart is that defect counts are integer numbers. So even though the calculated UCL = 7.1, in practice, it would be 7. You round to the nearest nonnegative integer value.

In the last section of this chapter, we will examine additional illustrations to practice your skill in creating and interpreting SPC charts. First, we need to examine one other aspect of interpreting control charts to ensure process quality. The process may be under control, but is it capable of producing the desired level of quality?

PROCESS CAPABILITY

A common misperception is that control limits are the same thing as specifications. Au contraire! Specifications represent what you *want* the process to do; control limits represent what the process *can* do. Specification limits, also called "tolerances," are extrinsic (set outside the process). Control limits are intrinsic to, or part of, the process.

Why is this important? Because you want to know if your process is capable of meeting specifications, especially if those specs came from a customer or the government—as in the case of net weight claims on packaging. There are four possible scenarios when comparing upper specification limits (USLs) and lower specification limits (LSLs) with upper and lower control limits:

1. The USL and LSL are outside of both the UCL and the LCL, which means your process is capable of operating within tolerances.
2. The USL and LSL are inside both the UCL and the LCL, demonstrating that tolerances are narrower than the process can reliably produce when under control.
3. The USL is less than the UCL, and the LSL is greater than the LCL. This means if the process is in control, it is likely to produce values greater than the upper specification.
4. The USL is greater than the UCL, and the LSL is less than the LCL. This indicates that you will have trouble meeting the lower specification.

Both scenarios 3 and 4 *might* be correctable by recentering the process.

These scenarios are illustrated in Figure 8-5. Think of USL-LSL as the *allowable* spread and UCL-LCL as the *actual* spread. Conceptually, if your

Figure 8-5 Sample Scenarios

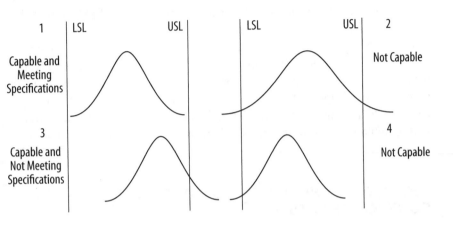

process is not capable of meeting specifications, you can recenter it and/or make changes to reduce process variability (a fun animation of changing this process is available at http://elsmar.com/Cp_vs_Cpk.html).

Mathematically, we use indices to indicate process capability, where MIN is the lowest value (minimum) in the MIN function's brackets:

$$C_p = (USL\text{-}LSL)/6\sigma$$
$$C_{pk} = min\ [(USL - \mu)/3\sigma, (\mu - LSL)/3\sigma]$$

This looks daunting, but it is really simple arithmetic. (I will spare you another poem though!)

Since process parameters μ and σ are typically unknown, we estimate that $\mu = \overline{X}$ and $\sigma = (A_2 \times \overline{R}) / 3$ (when control limits are $\pm3\sigma$ and we are using control charts for variables), as is typical when evaluating process capability. When C_p and $C_{pk} > 1.0$, the process is capable of meeting the allowable spread, as in scenario 1. Conversely, scenario 2 occurs if $C_p \leqq 1$. If $C_p \geqq 1$, but $C_{pk} \leqq 1$, that indicates the process should be recentered, as in scenarios 3 and 4.

Statistical thinking is an important part of managing for results, although some managers shy away from statistics.[5] As you can see though, while the theoretical foundation is profound, the actual calculation and interpretation of statistics in process control are quite simple. It takes a small amount of quantitative analysis to uncover objective, verifiable, defensible, and communicable insights that are critical to ensuring continuous process improvement.[6]

SPC takes a proactive approach to ensuring quality and elevating throughput by measuring during, not after, the process. It informs decisions about process improvements and adjustments. It reduces waste in a process by identifying the presence of assignable causes. Perhaps most importantly, it enables you to determine whether you can satisfy your customers' requirements.

TECHNIQUE: CREATING AND INTERPRETING CONTROL CHARTS

The focus of this chapter has been on creating and interpreting control charts, so in this section, we will extend that work with some additional examples. As an operations manager, it is unlikely that you will be developing these charts yourself, but the practice of creating them may enhance your statistical thinking.

Example 1: Chair Assembly

The Comfortable Wood Company (CWC) wants to use SPC to test its chairs, because it offers a 10-year quality guarantee with its furniture. One of the most important quality characteristics of a chair is that it does not wobble. To establish the initial control charts, 30 samples, each containing three chairs, were chosen from different shifts over several days of operation. In this example, CWC measures a variable—the wobble—in terms of degrees from level, using special instrumentation.

For SPC of variables, we use the $\overline{X}$ chart and R-chart. With $n = 3$, our factors are $A_2 = 1.02$, $D_4 = 0.00$, and $D_3 = 2.57$. Putting the sample data into a spreadsheet, with each sample taking one column, we calculate $\overline{X}$ and R for each sample—the overall grand mean = 0.52 and the average R = 0.51.

With a center line of 0.52, the control limits for the $\overline{X}$ chart are

$$UCL\overline{X} = 0.52 + (1.02 \times 0.51) = 1.04 \text{ degrees of wobble}$$
$$LCL\overline{X} = 0.52 - (1.02 \times 0.51) = 0.20 \text{ degrees}$$

Accordingly, the control limits for the R-chart are

$$UCL_R = 0.51 \times 0.00 = 0.00$$
$$LCL_R = 0.51 \times 2.57 = 1.31$$

with a center line of 0.51.

We can now plot the sample statistics on the $\overline{X}$ chart and R-chart to look for anomalies or trends. For example, the automatic saw for the legs might have dirt buildup or sawdust accumulation that would cause a change in the measurements. Vibrations from operations may put the drill out of alignment. Changes in temperature or humidity, general equipment deterioration, tool wear, or operator fatigue may also cause such a trend.

We also want to examine the process's capability. Our market research has shown that as long as the degrees of wobble are less than 0.75 degrees, the wobble is imperceptible to customers. That indicates that our USL is 0.75, and our LSL is 0.00. Calculating our capability indexes, using an estimate of $\sigma = (1.02 \times 0.51)/3 = 0.17$, we find that

$$C_p = (USL - LSL)/6\sigma = (0.75 - 0.00)/(6.00 \times 0.17) = 0.78$$

$$C_{pk} = \min\left[(USL - \mu)/3\sigma, (\mu - LSL)/3\sigma\right] = \min\left[(0.75 - 0.51)/(3.00 \times 0.17),\right.$$
$$\left.(0.51 - 0.00)/(3.00 \times 0.17)\right]$$

$$= \min\left[(0.53/0.51), (0.31/0.51)\right] = \min\left[0.47, 1.00\right] = 0.47$$

Therefore, we can see that while the process is in control, it is not capable of producing the desired quality. CWC management and engineering must revisit the design of the product and process to improve its capabilities.

Example 2: Candy Wrapping

The owner of Homemade Sweets knows it is important for each item produced to be individually wrapped before distribution. Each week, a random sample of 2,500 candies is taken, and the number of incorrectly wrapped candies is recorded. The results for a 12-week period are shown in Table 8-3.

In this case, the quality characteristic of interest is how well the candy is wrapped. This attribute can have just two possible values, correct and incorrect, so we know the best process control chart is a p-chart. The only

Table 8-3 Data for Example 2: Candy Wrapping

Sample Number	# Defects
1	15
2	12
3	19
4	2
5	19
6	4
7	24
8	7
9	10
10	17
11	15
12	3

Total = 147

real trick to this type of chart is to understand that the sample size is $n = 2,500$ and that we have $N = 12$ samples. To calculate the average fraction defective, or $\bar{p}$, we take the total number of defectives (147) and divide by the total number of observations (which is $n \times N = 2,500 \times 12 = 30,000$). Then $\bar{p} = 147/30,000 = 0.0049$.

With a center line of 0.0049, the $\pm 3\sigma$ control limits for the p-chart are

$$UCL_p = p + 3 \times \sqrt{[p(1 - p)/n]} = 0.0049 + 3\sqrt{[0.0049 \times (1 - 0.0049)/2,500]} = 0.0091$$
$$LCL_p = p - 3 \times \sqrt{[p(1 - p)/n]} = 0.0049 - 3\sqrt{[0.0049 \times (1 - 0.0049)/2,500]} = 0.0007$$

To determine whether the process is out of control, we need to calculate the value of p_i for each individual sample i (simply the number defective/n) and then plot these results on the control chart. In doing so, we can see that sample 7, with $p_7 = 24/2,500 = 0.0096$, is outside of the UCL of 0.0091.

If this scenario were to occur in practice, the owner would likely ask someone on the management team to explore the circumstances when sample

7 was taken. It might be determined that the recent lot of wrappers received from the supplier was out of specification. In that scenario, the wrappers would be replaced. Homemade Sweets would address the underlying issue with the supplier and make changes to the receiving department's procedures. After the problem was corrected, an analyst would recalculate the control limits.[7]

Example 3: Flooring Production

Underfoot Vinyl produces vinyl flooring used by apartment builders. The vinyl is mixed, pressed, cut, and rolled in a continuous process. Each day, the operator inspects a randomly selected cut of flooring as it goes into the roller and counts the number of blemishes in the cut. Table 8-4 shows the results from inspecting 15 rolls of vinyl flooring during a three-week period.

Table 8-4 Data for Example 3: Floor Blemishes

Sample Number	# Defects
1	12
2	8
3	16
4	14
5	10
6	11
7	9
8	14
9	13
10	15
11	12
12	10
13	14
14	17
15	15

Total = 190

The quality characteristic, blemishes, is a numerical count. That, of course, indicates that a c-chart should be used. There can be more than one blemish per roll. It is unclear how many blemishes a roll must have to be considered defective. (This is typically a judgment call by management, with input from customers and the marketing staff.) This makes a p-chart inappropriate, as there is neither a binary (defective/nondefective) evaluation nor a percentage of samples to meaningfully calculate.

For a c-chart, the $\bar{c}$ is the total number of defects divided by the number of samples. In this case, $\bar{c} = 190/15 = 12.7$ blemishes. The control limits are

$$UCL_c = \bar{c} + 3.0 \times \sqrt{\bar{c}} = 12.7 + 3.0 \times \sqrt{12.7} = 23.3$$
$$LCL_c = \bar{c} - 3.0 \times \sqrt{\bar{c}} = 12.7 - 3.0 \times \sqrt{12.7} = 2.0$$

Plotting the samples on the c-chart shows that the process is in control.

These illustrations are simplified. The intent here is to develop your statistical thinking and understanding of when SPC should be used and how to interpret the charts. In reality, you would have much more data to calculate and plot. Also keep in mind that in an organization pursuing Six Sigma, employees designated as green or black belts have more extensive practice in the development of control charts. However, the mechanics are still the same, regardless of the situation. The analysis of improbabilities is also the same, because the normal distribution does not change. What varies in actual applications is the appropriate action to take when an anomaly occurs. Should the manufacturing line be stopped? Should more random samples be taken for closer observation? That depends on the consequences of being out of control.

Application and Review

1. Think of a process you perform or manage. What are the assignable causes of variability in this process? What quality characteristic would you measure for this process?

2. Experiment with using Excel to generate each type of control chart. Make up your own data. If you are not comfortable with Excel, I suggest you consult the article at *Quality Digest*'s website (quality digest.com/apr99/html/excel.html). You can also look for templates on the Internet, such as the one available on the American Society of Quality's website (asq.org/learn-about-quality/data-collection -analysis-tools/overview/asq-control-chart.xls).

SUMMARY

Processes inherently have variability. Effective process control distinguishes between variability that is to be expected from variability that is triggered by one or more factors. Common causes of variation occur naturally in a process; assignable causes result from specific and correctable causes.

The theoretical foundation for statistical process control is the normal distribution invoked by the central limit theorem. By measuring samples produced by the process, you can evaluate whether the process is in control by looking for statistical improbabilities.

Control charts can be used for quality characteristics that are variables or attributes. Typically, control charts for variables use $\overline{X}$ and R-charts based on statistics of the sample measures. The most common control charts for attributes are p-charts for percent defective and c-charts for counts of defects.

Implementation considerations for SPC include what quality characteristics to measure, what sampling plan to use, and what risk level to assume. Establishing initial control charts is a trial-and-error process until the process is determined to be in control.

Creating SPC charts starts with the samples' statistics. The mean of the statistics is the center line of the chart. The upper and lower control limits are typically set at $\pm 3\sigma$ (that is, our estimate of $\pm 3\sigma$), respectively. Then the data are plotted in chronological order. To analyze the chart, we look for statistical improbabilities.

A process's capability to meet specifications is determined by comparing its allowable variance to its actual variance. By calculating capability indexes C_p and C_{pk}, we can determine whether the process is capable and centered.

Review Questions

1. Which of the following statements about the normal distribution is incorrect?
   a. It is defined by two parameters, μ and σ.
   b. It describes a wide range of naturally occurring phenomena.
   c. The probability density between one and two standard deviations from the mean changes, depending on the spread.
   d. It can be used to estimate other types of probability distributions.

2. **How are common causes different from assignable causes?**
    a. Assignable causes enable the manager to assign blame.
    b. Common causes are purely random.
    c. Common causes indicate that the process is out of control.
    d. Assignable causes are unavoidable.

3. **Which of the following is *not* one of the decisions to be made when implementing SPC?**
    a. Which rule of thumb you should use to identify improbable results
    b. What quality characteristic you should measure
    c. What your sampling plan is
    d. How much risk you are willing to accept for being wrong

4. **Which of the following guidelines should be considered when deciding where to take measurements in a process?**
    a. Where the cost of poor quality is greatest
    b. After a bottleneck
    c. Before a step that would obscure important quality characteristics
    d. a and c
    e. All of the above

5. **Which of the following factors is used to estimate the standard deviation, when using sample ranges, for an $\overline{X}$ chart?**
    a. 0.58
    b. A_2
    c. $\sqrt{\overline{c}}$
    d. C_{pk}

6. **Since the normal distribution is symmetrical, control charts are always symmetrical.**
    a. True
    b. False

7. **If a quality characteristic is being measured as either defective or nondefective, the correct SPC chart to use would be _____.**
    a. $\overline{X}$
    b. R
    c. p
    d. c

8. **If the tolerances fall within the UCL and LCL of a process, then we would consider the process to be capable.**
    a. True
    b. False

9. Referring back to Figure 8-5, your landscaping company's UCL for the c-chart is 7, and the LCL for the c-chart is 0. Adding to your previous sequence of 23 samples, you take 4 more. Which of the following sample counts would indicate that you may have assignable causes of variation?
   a. 5, 2, 1, 5
   b. 2, 3, 4, 5
   c. 2, 3, 3, 2
   d. 2, 5, 5, 1
10. When first establishing a process's control limits, you should use a different sample size to increase between-sample variations.
    a. True
    b. False

C H A P T E R

9

PROJECT DEFINITION FOR RESULTS

I would not give a fig for the simplicity this side of
complexity, but I would give my life for the simplicity
on the other side of complexity.

—OLIVER WENDELL HOLMES, JR.

As a child, you probably did not say, "When I grow up, I want to be a project manager," yet remarkably, that is what many of us become. Pinto and Kharbanda referred to project management as the "accidental profession," explaining that "having stumbled into the knowledge that project management has become a vital tool in their organizational processes, corporations must now learn how best to develop and use that tool."[1] Other than the "administrivia" (mail, messages, expense reports, and so on) that consumes a large part of the day, most professionals' work is organized as projects. They may not be called projects or explicitly follow project management processes, but they are still projects.

Much of what we have covered thus far is achieved by completing projects, such as developing a product or service, instituting a quality program, implementing a Six Sigma improvement, applying a new enterprise-wide information system, designing or reengineering a process, and establishing statistical quality control. What enables you to achieve your desired results—and figure out which way you ought to go—is a wide-ranging combination of management practices and techniques that comprise the field of project management.

After completing this chapter, you should be able to do the following:

- Describe the project management body of knowledge
- Identify project success factors and potential pitfalls
- Understand the tips, tricks, and traps of project definition
- Define a project in clear and concise terms

THE PROJECT MANAGEMENT BODY OF KNOWLEDGE

The *Project Management Institute (PMI)* is a professional organization focused on making project management intentional rather than accidental. To formalize project management as a profession, PMI offers initial and ongoing certification based on examinations and professional experience; ethical standards for public good; and codification of the project management body of knowledge *(PMBOK)*. With the increasing emphasis on project-based work in organizations, more companies value the credentialing of certified *project management professionals (PMPs)*.

Knowledge Areas

The PMBOK presents nine knowledge areas in project management that are common to various industry applications:[2]

- **Integration management:** Includes processes to ensure that the project elements are coordinated and includes project plan development and execution, as well as integrated change control.
- **Scope management:** Includes processes to ensure that the project includes all of the work required—and only the work required—to complete the project successfully. This includes scope planning, definition, verification, and change control.

- **Time management:** Includes the processes to ensure the timely completion of the project, such as activity definition, sequencing, and duration estimation for schedule development and control.
- **Cost management:** Includes processes to ensure that the project is completed within the approved budget, starting with resource planning and continuing through estimating, budgeting, and cost control.
- **Quality management:** Includes planning, assurance, and control processes to ensure that the project will satisfy the goals for which it was undertaken.
- **Human resource management:** Includes the processes required to make the most effective use of the people involved with the project through organizational planning, staff acquisition, and team development activities.
- **Project communications management:** Includes the processes needed for effective communications, such as stakeholder analysis and plan development, information distribution, performance reporting, and administrative closure.
- **Risk management:** Includes processes to maximize the probability and consequences of positive events and minimize the probability and consequences of events that are adverse to project objectives. This results from risk management planning, risk identification, risk analysis (quantitative and qualitative), risk response planning, and risk monitoring and control.
- **Procurement management:** Includes processes required to acquire goods and services to attain project scope, such as planning, solicitation, source selection, contract administration, and contract closeout.

Project Management Defined

In the context of this wide range of knowledge areas and processes, PMI's website defines a project as a "temporary endeavor undertaken to create a unique product or service." Let's deconstruct this definition to make some important points and offer some illustrations.

First, by being temporary, a project has a beginning and an end. Temporary does not necessarily mean short-term; a project may span several years. However, there is a clear point at which a project is over. For example, a business may work to develop a large information system, and the project—which encompasses needs analysis, design, development, testing and implementation—lasts more than two years. Once the application has been "put into production" and is being used and supported as part of normal business operations, the project is finished. Future enhancements may be made, but those would be considered different projects than the initial implementation.

The use of the term *endeavor* signals that all projects represent some risk. A successful completion is not guaranteed. Risk is a product of the probability of failure and the consequences and cost of that failure. The riskier the project, the more formality and control are needed in the project management process.

The result of any project is a unique one, meaning that it may be only slightly different from previous endeavors or that it may be entirely novel, in contrast to a manufacturing process designed to produce identical candy bars or tires or batches of paint. The product or service produced by a project may be something of commercial value or something for internal use, such as a process improvement or a strategic plan. Building houses from the same floor plan may be similar, but each situation is slightly different. Circumstances of site location, weather conditions, crew changes, and supply variations can all contribute to the uniqueness of each house and project. Improvements in the building process may arise from lessons learned on earlier construction projects.

In the same way, I view my classes as projects. I may teach operations management to M.B.A. students every fall, but each year is a unique experience. Just having a new set of students can make a remarkable difference! Add to that changes in examples, emphasis, and exercises, and I have further distinctions.

Each of these characteristics of a project determines how much formal project management should be needed—structured methodology, written communications, detailed schedules, budget tracking, and so on. Typically, the longer a project is, the riskier it is perceived to be, the more unique the result will be, and the more important it is to invest the necessary time and effort in formal project management. Practical considerations should determine how formally you should treat an effort. For example, haircuts have a clear beginning and end, have some risk associated with them, and create (sometimes *really*) unique results. Does the hairdresser create a written project definition and risk analysis? No, but a good stylist or barber starts with a clear discussion with the client to understand what the client wants and what the possible outcomes might be. The basic principles of project management are applicable, even if they are not explicitly applied in this situation.

PROJECT MANAGEMENT FOUNDATIONS

Building on scientific management, behaviorism, systems thinking, and contingency theory, project management is a synthesis of theory and application. Fundamentally, project management principles and processes are used to increase a project's probability of success—however that is measured. This is accomplished because good project management does the following:

- Manages complexity with explicit plans, controlled changes, risk management, and intentional communications
- Leverages expertise by identifying and acquiring specific resources at specific times, promoting team development, and distributing information
- Promotes organizational learning with clear project definitions, performance reporting, quality management, and administrative and contract closeouts
- Supports organic organizational structures by sequencing activities and scheduling work in a way that makes sense for the project, outside of the formal organizational hierarchy
- Prepares for risk response with plans to adjust for positive and negative effects outside the project
- Facilitates change within a project with scope, schedule, quality, and management controls that make it clear what the impact of changes will be. Stakeholder analysis and communications management also support the project team's ability to change.

Project management is systematic in approach, oriented to human factors, adaptable in uncertainty, and effective for interdependent activity coordination—in fact, it is a process. And in today's complex and dynamic business environment, it is a crucial management practice.

The techniques associated with project management have evolved since the beginning of civilization. Here are some specific milestones in that evolution:

- Construction works of antiquity, such as the Egyptian pyramids and the Great Wall of China
- Shipbuilding, such as the Spanish armada and the Swedish *Vasa*
- Large-scale product development, as in automobile production
- Resource tracking, like the Gantt chart used in World War I

- Process flow diagrams, such as those used in World War II
- The critical path method (CPM) developed by DuPont and the program evaluation and review technique (PERT) developed by the U.S Navy in the 1950s
- Personal computers and tracking software that have been widely available since the 1990s

As the complexity of society and business has grown, so too have the tools available to manage projects. The fundamentals have not changed, however—and in some cases, neither have the mistakes.

PROJECT SUCCESS FACTORS

What makes some projects succeed and some fail? While we may be inclined to point to a technological issue or personnel problem, study after study has shown that the key success factors for a project are (1) the clear definition of objectives; (2) a realistic schedule of activities; and (3) the true commitment of the project team, including the project's sponsor.[3] There are many different methodologies for project selection; just make sure you have these top three factors in place.

Certainly, the absence of technological or personnel issues is helpful, but it is not primary. Other contributing factors include top management support, client consultation, project control, well-defined communications, and contingency planning. Things will change as a project progresses. It is easier to manage those changes if you already have a good plan in place. As Gido and Clements describe it, good project management is "planning the work and then working the plan."[4]

It's really common sense. Without a clear definition of objectives, you are likely to run into "scope creep," where the expectations for the project are moving targets. You might also overlook some stakeholders' expectations. If you don't have a clear definition of what you are trying to accomplish, how can you possibly achieve it or expect other people to be committed to it? And if your project sponsor isn't deeply committed to the project, you are likely to run into conflicts with priorities, resource allocation, and issue resolution. These problems will spill over and cause schedule problems and delays.

As we have seen time and time again, common sense is not that common. The definition of a project is often neglected. Projects may be initiated as a result of a passing conversation. Workload pressures may lead people to feel that they don't have time for planning. Instructions may be vague or confusing. Or the definition that is created is a meaningless paper exercise. Yet nothing you do as the manager of a project will have a greater impact on project performance than defining the project clearly.

Project performance is usually measured in terms of whether the end result is delivered on time and within budget, but there is another important dimension of project performance to consider: the *perception* of performance. You may have done a fantastic job of running a promotional campaign project, but if the sponsor, customer, or client was expecting something else, the perceived performance will be low. When you think of customer satisfaction as a ratio of what is delivered to what was expected, it is easy to see how important it is to deal with expectations in the project management process. It is important to sustain a customer-oriented focus throughout the project.[5] This is achieved, in large part, by how the project is defined at the onset.

PROJECT DEFINITION

If you recall that a project is a temporary endeavor to create a unique product or service, then you are off to a good start in defining your particular project. What determines when the project starts? When does it end? What is it supposed to accomplish? Beyond this, you will want to know if any key assumptions should be made as the basis for further planning. Who will be involved? Do you know of any risks or issues at the onset of the project? Let's consider some illustrations of representative situations and potential pitfalls. The chapter will end with simple techniques to provide your projects with a strong start.

Illustrations

Imagine that you are a regional sales director for a pulp and paper company. You have a dozen salespeople who call directly on key customers and distributors in your region. You report to the vice president of sales. She calls to say she recently played golf with a buddy who heads up sales for a pharmaceutical firm and learned that his drug reps were using a contact management system for customer relationship management. During the conversation, she says, "I think we could really benefit from something like this. Get a few of your people together and look at what's out there. I'd like for us to be trying this out in your region before the end of the third quarter." You agree, and as the call ends, you feel a knot in the pit of your stomach.

First of all, you happen to know (from *your* golf buddies and from reading Chapter 6) that contact management and customer relationship management (CRM) systems are many orders of magnitude different in scope and complexity—and difficulty to implement. It is not clear what your boss really expects, much less what this project is supposed to accomplish. Also, your reps will howl over having to do staff work like this; they resist anything that takes them out of the field and away from customers. On top of that, you know that it's just a short leap from "trying this out in your region" to implementing it across the company. It is an overwhelming prospect.

You have several options. One is to procrastinate and hope the project will go away. Another is to contact someone you know in the IT department to see if CRM is on their horizon. You toy with the idea of sending a message out to your reps, asking what they are currently doing to keep track of their customer contacts—not just names and addresses, but problems, requests, personalized information, and so on. You could also follow up with your boss and ask for the name of her buddy, so you can garner the specifics directly from the source. You could also do a little research on the Internet to see if there are any useful product reviews. Each of these steps may help, but you still won't know what it is you are trying to accomplish. What should the end result be? How will you know it has been successful? Is there a budget for this? What if you need help from people other than those who report directly to you?

Without answers to these questions, you realize that your boss is (perhaps unintentionally) setting you up for failure. You decide to call her back to get more specifics. It is easy to take someone's vague idea and develop it the wrong way for the wrong reasons. Once you clarify what she wants to accomplish, you will be in a better position to determine your next best step.

Often, the next best step is for you to follow up with a written statement of work to make sure that you and your boss have the same understanding of the project's definition. It may be that what she really wants is to understand which customers could be encouraged to develop a closer partnership with executive involvement. Then the objective might be to increase the profitability of targeted accounts. On the other hand, she may want to look at records for customers who have not purchased from your company in the last six months to a year to find out why. Here, the goal might be to increase the percentage of repeat customers per quarter. This information may already be available in your organization without jumping into a CRM system.

Variations on this general scenario abound. A client asks for help in developing a balanced scorecard, and the scope shifts into reengineering some business processes without a contract renegotiation. A brand manager launches a new version of cereal and achieves a 0.5 percent share in the first three months, which might be a great success—except that the group executive was expecting 2 percent. A volunteer group of working parents stages a fund-raising event and raises $40,000 for their children's school, a wonderful accomplishment until they realize that it took more than 2,000 man-hours to do it. A team of programmers develops a tracking database for a customer call center, not realizing that the project sponsor expects them to train the customer reps and provide on-site support during the initial implementation.

The Bottom Line

These illustrations show that unless you know what the "bottom line" of a project is supposed to be, you will probably not achieve it. While technically a good project finishes on time, in budget, and with the intended results, if those results are not clearly defined in business terms (that is, the bottom line), the project cannot succeed. In my experience, if the project is not correctly defined, then the schedule and budget are probably wrong too. Consider that customer satisfaction is really a ratio of deliverables to expectations. We tend to focus our energies on the deliverables and neglect the expectations. Neglected expectations often grow, making it difficult for the deliverables to exceed what is desired (you want the ratio to be ≥ 1).

The solution is a simple but powerful approach that encourages understanding and collaboration. It is useful in managing expectations and ensuring sponsor support. The technique of project definition is foundational to all of the other processes in project management. The following method is a practical approach that focuses on results, not paperwork.

TECHNIQUE: DEVELOPING A STATEMENT OF WORK

A *statement of work* (*SOW*) captures the essence of a project in one page. Clear and concise, it promotes a common understanding *within* the project team and *among* the stakeholders of the project. Most important, it provides an enduring vision of the project's intended purpose.

Aspiring for the simplicity on the far side of complexity, as described in our opening quote, certain elements are key ingredients for a SOW: *scope definition, objectives, key stakeholders, assumptions,* and *issues.*

Scope Definition

This introductory paragraph often starts with "The purpose of this project is to . . ." and describes the specific deliverables that should result from the work. It should be clear as to what the scope does and does not include, as well as when the project begins and ends. In some cases, geographical and organizational boundaries may be relevant. For example, as the pulp and paper sales director in our example, you may determine the following:

> The purpose of this project is to identify former customers and understand why they no longer purchase from our company. The customer base to be used in the analysis is from the southeast region. Work will entail identifying lapsed customers, calling and interviewing contacts in those organizations, and developing a Pareto analysis of the key issues. The results of the analysis, with recommendations for improvements, will be presented to the executive team by the end of the second quarter.

Objectives

This section really has two parts. The first is the primary objective, or the reason for undertaking the project. The scope explains the *what* of the project; objectives cover the *why*. The primary objective is paramount; if you cannot accomplish this main objective, you might as well not bother doing the project. Keep in mind that you want a measurable, bottom-line primary objective. For example, if the purpose of the project is to launch a new product (what), the primary objective is to make money (why), defined in terms of product contribution, market share, or overall revenue.

The second part of this section contains the secondary objectives, which are typically expected benefits. They contribute to the project's impact but are not sufficient to determine its success. For example, you might expect that the product launch will create new opportunities for cross-marketing with other products. While that is not the primary reason to go to the expense of launching a new product, it is certainly an attractive benefit. When possible, these objectives should be measurable as well. I recommend bulleted, complete sentences for the secondary objectives to keep the SOW concise.

In the pulp and paper example, the primary objective might be expressed as "To develop a plan to increase customer retention by 20 percent," or "To develop a plan to have 100 former customers return in the next six months." It is a little tricky when the project purpose is really to develop a plan, but you should still have your eye on what the bottom line of the plan is. You should also be explicit about the target response rate from past customers, because it is unlikely that they will all want to speak with you. It is important to note that, when developing a plan, one possible result may be that you find the initiative to be planned is not feasible. The primary objective might be to squeeze three ounces of blood from a pound of turnips in one day. It's a measurable and well-specified objective to be sure, but it is totally impractical.

Key Stakeholders

People pay attention to documents that have their names on them. It is prudent to identify the project sponsor(s), the project leader, team members (by name, if known; otherwise by role), and important people who have a vested interest in the conduct and/or outcome of the project. This list represents the foundation of your communications plan, so you know who should be kept apprised of project developments. For your customer retention initiative, you want to ensure that your boss (or her boss) is the executive sponsor. You are likely the project leader, since you will not want to take away from your sales force's customer time. The other regional sales directors are likely stakeholders, as are department heads for areas that have customer contact.

Assumptions

This is one of the more challenging components of a SOW, because our assumptions are usually tacit, and we are trying to make them explicit here. It helps if you are developing the SOW as part of a team, because it is easier to spot assumptions that are expressed by other people. This section is useful for addressing questions about resource availability and project approach. For the product launch example, you might assume that "the Web management department is ready to create a new, interactive set of pages" to support your launch. In the case of the customer retention project, one assumption may be that "the southeast region's customer base is representative of that in other regions." You might also make an explicit assumption that "the necessary reports are easily obtained from existing systems."

Issues

These concerns are beyond the ability of the project team to control but can have an impact on the project's outcome. Typically, this section is used to flag issues for the sponsor's attention, such as timing conflicts, resource constraints, and project risks. In the case of a product launch, it might highlight a concern about timing, such as coinciding with a busy period for the company or an issue with the advertising agency. For the sales director who is chasing down old customers, one issue might be whether "there should be a budget for short-term remediation efforts (solving the specific problem that drove that customer away)."

Other

Some companies require other topics that must be addressed in more detail during project definition, such as resource requirements, budget, or risk analysis. While these are all worthy considerations that you should address in your planning, I do not consider them to be essential in the initial SOW, as they can make it cumbersome.

Be careful of making your SOW overly long or wordy. Sometimes a second page is really needed—but never more than that. Why? Because the longer it is, the less likely people are to read it. If they haven't read it, you have lost the common understanding and support needed for project success. Here are some additional suggestions:

- Use bullets for every section except the Scope Definition to keep the SOW clear and concise.
- Make sure the objectives are measurable so the criteria for success are unambiguous.
- Write each bullet in the "Assumptions" and "Issues" sections in complete sentences to ensure complete thoughts.
- Put required details in a separate document as an attachment for the SOW, to avoid clutter.
- Treat complex projects as programs with subprojects, each with its own SOW, to achieve a useful level of perspective.

Remember that without clear business direction, there is no way to determine whether the project is successful. The clear business direction should describe the impact of the project in quantifiable terms. A common pitfall is to "express a project objective as the delivery of a new or revised system . . . [whereas] a simple business statement . . . is easy to understand; it also provides the basis for determining project benefits and measuring project success."[6]

The process for developing SOWs is flexible. Given some sense of direction from an executive order, committee charge, or some other charter, you (the project leader) develop a draft SOW. This can be done in isolation or with members of the project team. Developing the SOW as a group takes longer, but it can be an effective way to initiate team building and involvement. The draft should be circulated to the people who participated in its development. It helps to take a second look at the document to assess whether it fulfills the necessary criteria:

- It is clear, even to the reader who was not in the room when it was written.
- The scope is defined so that it is clear what the project work will cover and when the project will be considered complete.
- The objectives are measurable and realistic.
- It is complete, including key assumptions, issues, and stakeholders.
- It is concise and limited to one or two legible pages.

Once the draft is polished, it should be presented to the project sponsor for his or her commitment and approval. Any changes at this point should be recirculated to the team and confirmed with the sponsor in writing. The final SOW should be an enduring document that serves as a touchstone for developing further project plans, indoctrinating new project team members, addressing scope changes, and resolving priority disputes. A sample SOW is presented in Figure 9-1.

This example describes a project to organize a silent auction for a vocational services organization. Note that the scope statement delineates the auction from other activities at the gala. Also note that the start and end points of the auction project are specified and are *not* the same as the start and end points of the event. The primary objective is to raise a targeted amount of money. The key stakeholders, including the sponsor, are identified by name. Assumptions and issues are explicit. The entire SOW fits on one 8½ × 11-inch page.

Sometimes the SOW is all you need for a successful project. But usually it's the first step in a process of defining, assigning, and scheduling the work to be done. Remember, the extent of formal project management should

Figure 9-1   Sample Statement of Work (SOW)

Vocational Services Gala Auction
Project Description
Revised August 30, 2007

SCOPE

The purpose of this project is to organize a silent auction to benefit the
Vocational Services South (VSS). The auction will be held in conjunction
with the Vocational Services Gala on the evening of Thursday, November
29, 2007. The project begins with a planning meeting with the Gala committee in early September, to discuss the Gala as a whole, including the
theme and the lessons learned. The scope of the pre-Gala activities for this
project includes the solicitation and collection of donations and consigned
items as well as the tracking and merchandising of them. At the Gala, we
will administer the bidding process, collect the payments, and transfer the
goods. Tasks after the Gala will include returning any remaining items,
sending thank-you notes and acknowledgments to donors, and noting suggestions for improvement. All work on the Gala Auction should be completed by Friday, December 13, 2007.

OBJECTIVES

The primary objective of the Auction is to raise $XX to benefit Vocational
Services South (VSS). Other objectives include:

- Raise the awareness of Vocational Services's mission to "build lives,
  families, and communities one job at a time" in the community, by
  contacting at least 10% more prospects than last year.
- Encourage greater participation in the Gala with 20% more auction-
  able items.
- Establish a planning template for future Gala functions.

PROJECT TEAM

The volunteer auction chair is Linda. The Vocational Services liaison is
Ivey. Other auction committee members are Barbara, Rita, Julia, and Bob.

The Gala chair is Joy. The executive sponsor for this project is Vocational Services CEO Jim.

ASSUMPTIONS
- Vocational Services has a secured area in which to store the donated items.
- We are not having a live auction as well.
- There will be plenty of tables and space in which to merchandise the donated items at the Gala.

CONCERNS
- It would simplify things if people could take their winnings with them from the Gala. However, we will need to set up a process to receive their payments.
- Security is also a consideration, especially if we get more valuable items on consignment.

be determined by the risks of the project and, of course, your organization's requirements. The less control you have over the work to be done, the more you need a project plan.

Considerations for Formal Planning

As with many aspects of management, there are trade-offs in formalizing project planning. Like the old joke "I don't have time to go to time management training," project planning can take more time than it is worth. Developing a meaningful plan and maintaining it during the project progression are time-intensive. On the other hand, planning greatly improves your probability of success. Therefore, the trade-off decision should be based on project *risk*.

Sources of risk can be technical hurdles beyond the project team's skill set, environmental factors beyond the team's control, or organizational politics that go over the project sponsor's head. A crisis elsewhere in the organization may call for all hands on deck and derail your project's schedule. A constraint presented by a supplier or a customer may limit your ability to produce the desired results. Sometimes risks can be anticipated and plans made to mitigate those risks.

I have found that one of the biggest risks is resource unavailability, that is, a key person is not available when you need him or her. In terms of the theory of constraints (Chapter 7), this person is a bottleneck that restricts your ability to produce according to plan. This seems to be endemic to companies that have several simultaneous projects with part-time resources. In such a scenario, Goldratt suggests that you examine the "critical chain" that links all of the projects to manage the interdependencies outside of the individual projects.[7]

If you are the only resource on the project or you have control over the resources needed, you may not need a project plan but still find it helpful for scheduling purposes. I have also found it useful to have a detailed plan when I negotiate with other managers about resources they control. My rule of thumb is that if the project lasts longer than a month, has more than three project team members, or contains more than 50 tasks to be done, I will develop a networked project schedule (a formalized project plan).

A formalized project plan takes the work to be done and divides it into pieces. The number of pieces should depend on how closely the project manager needs to monitor the work. For example, if you are doing some work on your home, you might have simply identified one part of it as "Paint the kitchen." If your spouse is doing the painting, you might develop a more granular (detailed) list of work:

- Bring paint samples home.
- Decide on the color as a family.
- Purchase paint.
- Prepare the room to be painted.
- Paint the kitchen.
- Restore the room.

Just having the list broken out like this can help you with the planning (for example, you know you must pick up the paint by Friday so the painting can be done over the weekend) and the division of labor, such as who is responsible for preparing the room to be painted.

Certainly, you can achieve an even greater level of detail, and it might be warranted. Another corollary to "you can't manage what you don't measure" is "match the level of detail to the desired amount of management control." If your project requires more attention to detail, then you want to develop a work breakdown structure, a technique that we apply in the next chapter.

Application and Reflection

1. What work do you currently have that you might now consider to be a project, using the definition given in this chapter?
2. Imagine you are a brand manager for a toy company. Think of a new toy that you are responsible for launching. Draft the SOW for that project.
3. Go to the Project Management Institute's website (pmi.org) and find out the options and requirements to become certified as a Project Management Professional (PMP). Would the PMP credential be useful to you?

SUMMARY

Project management is a process and practice that has developed over centuries, incorporating the best thinking in the field. It encompasses a wide range of knowledge areas, including integration, scope, time, cost, quality, human resources, project communications, risk, and procurement management.

Projects are most likely to succeed when they have clear objectives, a realistic schedule, and executive sponsorship. These factors provide clarity and engender commitment in the project team.

When defining a project, it is essential to be explicit about the project's scope and ultimate goals. Success should be defined in measurable, bottom-line terms. This ensures a common understanding of the project's purpose among the project team and other stakeholders, and it is especially helpful in managing the expectations of the project's customers.

A statement of work is a one-page document that can provide an at-a-glance view of the project's scope and objectives. It is also helpful in explicating assumptions and constraints and alerting the project sponsor and/or customer to potential issues that could impact the project's progression.

The SOW may be all you need to get the project going on the right track. Remember that the extent of formal project management should be determined by the risks of the project and, of course, your organization's requirements. The less control you have over the work to be done, the more you need project management.

Review Questions

1. Project management's usefulness to operations management is limited to Six Sigma initiatives.
   a. True
   b. False
2. Which of the following is *not* one of the knowledge areas identified by the Project Management Institute?
   a. Time management
   b. Risk management
   c. Systems management
   d. Project communications management
3. The integration management knowledge area includes processes for all of the following *except* _____.
   a. interracial relations
   b. project plan development
   c. change control
   d. coordinated execution
4. A project is defined as a _____ to create a _____ product or service.
   a. operational process; onetime
   b. long-term endeavor; new
   c. temporary endeavor; unique
   d. integration management; quality
5. Project management manages complexity with explicit plans, controlled changes, risk management, and intentional communications.
   a. True
   b. False

6. Which of the following statements about project success is *false*?
   a. Executive sponsorship for a project is crucial, particularly to get past roadblocks.
   b. The best projects naturally grow—or have scope creep—because the customer is so satisfied.
   c. The commitment of the project team can mean the difference between success and failure.
   d. Successful projects start with a clear and realistic plan, even though things do not necessarily turn out as anticipated.

7. Customer satisfaction occurs when the customer's expectations are greater than the deliverables.
   a. True
   b. False

8. In a statement of work, the scope describes the _____ and the objectives identify the _____ of the project.
   a. how; when
   b. what; where
   c. why; how
   d. what; why

9. Objectives should be _____.
   a. explicit
   b. measurable
   c. numerous
   d. a and b
   e. All of the above

10. Which of the following statements about SOWs is *false*?
    a. Assumptions highlight potential problems beyond the control of the project team.
    b. The scope describes the beginning and end of a project in terms of time, place, and results.
    c. You should have only one bottom-line, primary objective.
    d. Only powerful stakeholders should be included.

10

PROJECT PLANNING

A journey of a thousand miles must begin
with a single step.

—LAO-TZU

ormal project planning and scheduling, beyond an initial statement of work (SOW), can go a long way toward increasing the
probability of successfully completing the project. After completing this chapter, you should be able to do the following:

- Identify *work packages* and develop a *work breakdown structure*
- Develop and analyze a *network model*
- Estimate *task durations*
- Schedule a project using the *critical path method*
- Relate the *theory of constraints* to project scheduling
- Interpret a *Gantt* chart

WORK BREAKDOWN STRUCTURE

In the last chapter, we concluded that if your project requires more attention to detail to manage it effectively, then you need to develop a work breakdown structure (WBS). This is the first step in project planning and scheduling. As the name suggests, you break a project into manageable pieces. Think of the project as a boulder that you have to move out of your yard. The boulder is too heavy and big for you to carry, so you find a friend with a pickax, and he breaks the boulder into large rocks. Those still might be too much for you to handle. You call on another friend who has a sledgehammer, and he comes over and helps you pound the rocks into stones that you can carry.

In the same way, you use a WBS to take a monolithic project and break it into assignable tasks for the project team. A WBS identifies the work to be done in a systematic, hierarchical way. A good one clearly defines actions with verbs and helps everyone involved understand the project's vision and progression, essentially preparing the project team for scheduling. It makes the project less overwhelming and is also a good way to involve ad hoc members in the project, leveraging their experience and expertise in the planning phase. The main purpose of using a WBS, however, is to cover everything in the project that takes time (tasks, communications, approvals, delivery lead times, and so on).

Generally, developing a WBS is best done with the project team, whose members are all in the same room, seeing and hearing the same information. I like to use a flip chart and sticky notes rather than a computer. I feel that the paper-based approach is easier for people to follow and keeps everyone more engaged in the planning. The project leader or facilitator walks the team through the process, documenting as they go. (Later, the plan can be entered into a computer program.) The process is fairly dynamic, so the sticky notes make it easy to adjust. Again, the idea is to capture everything that takes time. At this point, we are not concerned with durations, responsibilities, or dependencies.

Phases are common in technology implementation, construction projects, and process design or improvement. Typically, the progression of phases starts with requirements analysis, then moves to design, development, testing, and implementation—or some variation thereof. Phased projects will often have a *milestone* to mark the end of each phase, such as a decision point (go/no go), a project review with the sponsor (approval for further funding), a tangible outcome (an erected building frame), or a report (budgeted versus actual spending).

Deliverable projects are those that produce several different results. For example, a wedding project might be broken down into deliverables, including arrangements for the bridal party, church, reception, honeymoon, and gifts. Each of these would have a different set of tasks and results. Ultimately, the desired results are to have the right people in the right attire in the right place at the right time.

If the project is considered level 0 (in terms of detail), then level 1 is usually defined in terms of "work packages," i.e., project phases or deliverables. (Some people try to define it by department, but that is a parochial view that can create gaps in the planning.) Continuing with the wedding illustration, the work packages (as defined by deliverables) can be broken into smaller pieces, which can be called level 2. Sometimes level 2 is as far as you need to go, and you can jump right into specific tasks that need to be done. Other times, though, it is helpful to break the packages into even smaller activities (level 3). In our wedding example, you might want to break the arrangements down by bridesmaids, groomsmen, and accommodations, since different people are likely to be responsible for each of those activities.

This segmentation continues until you get to the level of the actual tasks. Personally, I have never gone beyond level 4, but I imagine government projects could warrant more detail. Extremely complex projects are typically considered to be programs, an amalgamation of subsidiary projects managed by different project leaders and overseen by a program director. Large-scale system implementations, such as those described in Chapter 6, might be considered programs, with individual projects to address the data, programming, processes, and people involved.

A WBS might be constructed like an inverted tree (an organization chart) or as an indented list (outline format). I find that the tree works best in the planning session, and the indented list is useful for computer input. Using an outline form in the planning session encourages linear thinking, and important thoughts can be lost because they are "out of order."

The idea is that as you are developing the work breakdown structure, you identify things you might otherwise overlook. In this example, when you mention hiring a photographer, someone might note that you are missing the task of buying disposable cameras for the tables. Thinking of the tables would remind you that you need to make seating arrangements once the guest list is finalized. Seating arrangements leads to the need to make place cards. This is what I mean by the process being dynamic; even though it is a systematic methodology, ideas can surface randomly, triggering changes as you plan.

To round out the example, an abridged version of the same WBS is shown in Figure 10-1, using the indented list format. Even though I did not use level 2 activities for the church ceremony, I still numbered the tasks as being on level 4. Remember, the idea is to identify the work to be done, so do not let the project team become preoccupied with labeling.

When the project team thinks it is finished breaking down the work, it is a good idea to consider the following questions:

- Are the WBS elements uniquely assignable to an individual who is responsible for completing them? (Otherwise, you may not have the right level of detail.)
- Do the activities begin with a verb? (This helps to ensure that you are defining tasks.)
- Do the activities have beginning and ending points? (If not, it may be unclear as to what is to be done.)
- Are all the elements that take time included? (You might have overlooked waiting times, such as for alterations on a wedding dress.)
- Is quality built into the WBS with testing, revision cycles, feedback loops, and so on? (This is a good management practice!)
- Is the WBS sufficient for achieving the project objectives as stated in the SOW? (You want to ensure that you have a feasible plan with a strong chance of success.)

These questions may help you and your team identify some tasks you have overlooked. This is an especially good time to go back and consider whether any specific risks require focused attention.[1]

When you are *really* done with the WBS, everyone on the project team should have a good idea of exactly what has to be done to achieve the project's objectives. While this exercise is a useful process in and of itself, it is usually a precursor to scheduling the project plan.

PROJECT SCHEDULING

At this point, you have a glorified to-do list, which is necessary but probably not sufficient to complete the project. To coordinate activities and leverage

Figure 10-1   Excerpt of WBS in Indented List

Wedding (Level 0)

1. Bridal Party (Level 1)

   1.1. Bridesmaids (Level 2)

      1.1.1.   Decide on number in wedding party (Level 3)

      1.1.2.   Confirm bridesmaid selection

      1.1.3.   Decide on bridesmaid dresses

      1.1.4.   Arrange for bridesmaid dresses

      1.1.5.   Select thank-you gifts for the bridesmaids

   1.2. Groomsmen

      1.2.1.   Agree to the number in the wedding party

      1.2.2.   Confirm groomsmen selection

      1.2.3.   Agree to tux style

      1.2.4.   Tell groomsmen what to order

      1.2.5.   Select thank-you gifts for the groomsmen

   1.3. Accommodations

      1.3.1.   Check out local hotels . . .

2. Church ceremony

      2.1.1.   Meet with the pastor . . .

3. Reception . . .

4. Honeymoon . . .

5. Gifts . . .

      5.1.1.   Decide if/where to register

      5.1.2.   Make gift selections

      5.1.3.   Write thank-you notes

part-time resources, you will want to develop a schedule for the project. Also, your project's sponsor might have given you a deadline that may or may not be realistic. You will not know until you have a project schedule.

To create a schedule, you have to know the logical dependencies and durations of the tasks. In our wedding example, you cannot finalize the seating plan before the invitations are mailed; it is not a logical sequence. You also want to avoid situations like the flowers being delivered a week before they are needed. By incorporating logic and expected durations into the plan, you can develop a schedule that indicates when activities should start, how long they should take, and what should follow when they are completed. You will know where you have flexibility in your plan and whether a delay in one activity will delay the overall completion of the project. This is accomplished through the effective use of network models.

Network Models

A well-developed project schedule is more than just dates on a calendar. For one thing, a calendar does not reflect the logical sequence of activities. In addition, each activity has a remarkable amount of information associated with it, such as how long it will take, who is assigned to do it, and what other activities depend on its completion. You need a better way to capture this kind of information.

Network models are powerful and fairly intuitive tools. Like any model, a network model is a representation. In project scheduling, you use a network model to represent activities and relationships. Why is this approach especially useful?

- It captures the logical flow of activities.
- It simulates/visualizes the project as you plan.
- It helps you anticipate problems and consider contingencies.
- It enables you to attach information (such as durations and resources) to activities.
- It facilitates control and schedule changes.
- It provides a framework for project analysis.

Obviously, while a list of dates may be appropriate for small, simple projects, a network model provides the project team with a better way to plan and manage substantial projects.

Network models have two elements, nodes and links. They can be used for a wide range of applications beyond project management (for example, our process flow diagrams are really a special form of a network model). Depending on the application, the nodes and links mean different things.

Activity-on-Node Diagrams

For our purposes, we will focus on what the Project Management Institute refers to as the "precedence diagramming method," more generally referred to as *activity-on-node* (*AON*) diagrams. The method has several elements:

- *Nodes* represent the activities identified in the WBS.
- The links are drawn as arrows that connect immediate predecessors and successors and indicate a time sequence.
- Two activities that have a predecessor/successor relationship are *sequential*.
- Two or more independent activities that can be done at the same time are *parallel*.

There is a remarkable richness to this approach. Many details can be captured in the node, such as the activity description and duration, planned/actual start and finish times, resource assignments, activity responsibility, and cost centers.

The way the arrows are drawn also conveys meaning. If you picture the node as a rectangle, then the left side of the box is the start of the activity, and the right side is its finish. In this way, there are four ways to represent the logical relationship between two activities (A and B).

- **Finish-to-start (FS):** B can start as soon as A is finished. This represents the cleanest handoffs between activities and is the easiest to schedule. For our wedding example, the bride can order flowers (activity B) as soon as the date is set (activity A).
- **Start-to-start (SS):** B can start after A starts, usually with a lag time or delay between starts. In this example, B might be the preparation of place cards, which can start after A starts, once replies have begun to come in, perhaps with a *lag time* of a week to allow for mail delivery.
- **Finish-to-finish (FF):** This is unlikely and awkward; since we are using a commonsense approach, that is all I will say about it.
- **Start-to-finish (SF):** This is even worse than FF—don't even try it!

Seriously, in the last two cases, you are better off redefining the activities to use an FS or SS arrow. For example, for staging a symphonic production, you might try to define one activity as "Warm up the orchestra" and another as "Adjust the lighting." The thought here is that there is an SF relationship: the orchestra must start warming up before the stage manager can finish the lighting adjustments. It is much simpler to have an activity "Take stage positions" as a predecessor to both warming up and adjusting the lighting. Otherwise, your diagram will be convoluted, and it will be hard to analyze changes in the network.

The main alternative approach to network models for project scheduling is known as *activity-on-arrow/arc* (*AOA*) diagrams, also referred to as the arrow diagramming method. In this type of network model, the role of the node and the arrows (or arcs) are inverted; the nodes represent a point in time, the arrows represent the activities. I eschew this approach for several reasons, mostly because AOA relies on dummy activities for multiple predecessors, making the network extremely complicated and hard to analyze. It also uses only finish-to-start dependencies. I mention it because it is used for government work, in part because the scheduling algorithm for this model incorporates uncertainty in durations.

The program *evaluation and review technique* (*PERT*) uses optimistic, pessimistic, and most likely estimates of durations. In my experience, though, three estimates are not better than one. If a great deal of uncertainty exists in the project, then the project team should have regular updates to add detail and change the durations as needed.

Activity-on-Node Process

Returning to the AON development process, note that the AON must be bounded; that is, it must have a starting node and a finishing node. You might think of the starting node as pushing the activities to start as soon as possible and the ending node pushing back to keep the activities from being late. This logical "compression" is essential for schedule development.

Both the Start and Finish nodes have zero duration. You may also want to identify milestones in your project, which would also be nodes with zero duration. Other than the Start and Finish nodes, every node and milestone must have at least one predecessor and one successor. You do not want to have any "hanging danglers," or activities that are only partially connected without any compression!

The process of building the network is straightforward. Begin with Start and ask yourself, "Given where I am now (at time = 0), what can I start?" You will likely find that you *can* start several activities right away, even though you may choose not to do so. Remember that this is a model of the activities' relationships, so let the logic of those relationships dictate your node placement. Connect any activity that can be started (meaning it does not have any logical predecessors) to the Start node. At this point, you and the project team can add additional activities as warranted by working through iterations of these steps:

1. Assume that every activity connected in the diagram so far is completed.
2. Determine what can be done next.
3. Connect eligible activities to the existing network.
4. Repeat until all of the activities from your WBS have been connected.

At this point, check to make sure that every activity has a successor. If there is no logical successor to an activity, then connect it with the Finish node.

AON Example

Let's walk through a small example to illustrate the process. Assume that the activities and relationships for a project are as shown in Table 10-1. Although you are given the successor relationships, you have to infer the predecessor relationships, such as A has no predecessor, B is preceded by A, C has no predecessors, D is preceded by both B and C, and so on. To build the network, apply steps 1 through 4 in the following iterations.

Iteration 1
1. **Assume that every activity connected in the diagram so far is completed.** None.
2. **Determine what can be done next.** At time = 0, activities A and C can start right away, because they have no predecessors.
3. **Connect eligible activities to the existing network.** Activities A and C are connected to the Start node.
4. **Repeat until all the activities have been connected.**

Table 10-1   A Network Diagram Example

Activity	Successor(s)
A	B, E
B	D
C	D
D	E, F
E	G
F	G, H
G	None
H	None

Iteration 2

1. **Assume that every activity connected in the diagram so far is completed.**
2. **Determine what can be done next.** Assuming that both A and C are completed, only B can be started.
3. **Connect eligible activities to the existing network.** The only predecessor for activity B is A, so connect B with an arrow starting at A.
4. **Repeat until all of the activities have been connected.**

With A, B, and C finished, D can be done next. With A, B, C, and D finished, both E and F can be started. Once A, B, C, D, E and F are completed, then G and H can be started. With all of the activities connected, you can see that neither G nor H has a successor, so their finish edges are connected to the Finish node. The resulting diagram is presented in Figure 10-2. At this point, you are ready for the next step, adding the dimension of time.

Duration Estimation

The duration estimate plans for the elapsed time between the start and finish of an activity. *Elapsed* is the key word; this is not a measure of effort. For example, connecting with someone on the phone may take 30 minutes of actual time, but it usually requires two days of elapsed time to allow for telephone tag.

Figure 10-2   Sample AON Network

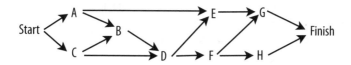

When estimating, I suggest that you use the "normal" time, or the duration associated with the most cost-effective use of resources. You can decide if extreme measures need to be taken, such as working overtime or hiring temporary staff, after you have a project schedule; for now, you can assume you have enough time. It helps with project team morale if the team members are the ones doing the estimating. Go through the project, activity by activity, and ask the following questions:

- **Who has responsibility for this activity?** This does not mean the person who will actually *do* the task; it might be a manager who has the responsibility and authority to assign resources to perform the task. Regardless, you want one name or set of initials associated with that node. If no one claims it, then it is the project manager's responsibility until it is assigned to someone else.
- **How long will it take to complete this activity once it is started?** The person responsible should provide the estimate, considering relevant constraints, assumptions, resource requirements and capabilities, historical information, and expert judgment. In some industries such as construction, tabulated values of standard times are available.

I try to walk the team through this process quickly; precise estimates are not necessary at this point. It is better for an activity duration to be wrong than for the activity to be forgotten! Do not let the planning get bogged down at this point.

In "working days," estimates of a week typically mean five days; a month is twenty. If someone feels that an activity will last longer than a month, I segment that activity into smaller pieces for greater accountability; the end of one segment serves as a checkpoint so the team does not wait until the last minute to start the entire task.

Sometimes, detailed discussion is warranted. For example, it may be necessary to determine the approach to the activity before its duration can be estimated. Make sure that assumption is noted in the project's communication records, e.g., status updates, meeting summaries, or SOW.

Another point of discussion might be the need for contingency reserves in certain activities. Both *The Critical Chain* author Eliyahu Goldratt and I think this is generally a bad idea. He argues that the contingency should be reserved at the project level. When you assign it to a task, that time is lost, even if the task did not require it.[2] I prefer to schedule the worst-case scenario—to see how bad it might be—and then (optimistically) bring the project in early.

When a team member is struggling with an estimate, you first want to ensure that the activity scope is clear. If it is, offer ranging/shrinking limits. For example, as the project manager (PM), you would have a conversation with your team member (TM) that goes something like this:

PM: Do you think you can get it done in a day?
TM: Oh, no. It will take longer than that.
PM: Well, is it something that will need two weeks?
TM: It shouldn't. Let's give it a week.

Failing that, a guess (also known as a "historical estimate") will suffice at this point. You can correct inaccuracies with downstream adjustments later in the project.

Something else to consider in duration estimation is whether you expect to encounter learning curves (see Chapter 7). This can be a significant consideration when you add inexperienced people to a project. "Up-to-speed learning," or the time it takes to become fully effective, is especially pronounced in white-collar projects such as large-scale systems development.[3] In the same way, there is a cost associated with "time to teach," as the more experienced members provide the guidance needed.

TECHNIQUE: CRITICAL PATH METHOD

Once you have a completed network model and tasks that have defined responsibilities and estimated durations, the next step is to develop the schedule. The *critical path method* (*CPM*), developed by the DuPont Corporation, is something that can be done by hand and with the project team's participation. You perform what is called the "forward pass," determining the earliest time when the activities and the projects can be finished. Then you make the "backward pass," starting at the project deadline and considering the latest point at which each activity can start and finish without delaying the overall project.

CPM Process

First you perform the forward pass. The Start node has no duration. Its earliest possible start and completion are 0. For each of its successors, the earliest possible start is 0; the earliest possible finish is at the end of the activity's duration.

For each activity, determine the early times. The earliest possible start of an activity is the latest of its predecessors' earliest possible finishes. Record both early start and early finish times on the node. Repeat this through the network all the way to the finish node.

Next, you perform the backward pass. The Finish node has no duration either. Its latest possible completion (or start) may be set equal to its earliest possible completion or to some target deadline. For each of its predecessors, the latest possible completion is the same as the Finish node's latest possible start. Subtract the activity's duration from its latest possible finish to find its latest possible start. Record both the latest start and latest finish times on the node. Repeat this through the network all the way to the Start node. The latest possible finish of an activity is the earliest of its successors' latest possible starts.

Now identify the critical path(s). The critical path is the path of longest duration from start to finish—not necessarily the most important path of activities—in the network. It determines the project's duration. Note that there can be more than one critical path. What makes a path critical is that any delay on that path will delay project completion. That means that to shorten the project's duration, you have to shorten all of the critical paths.

Calculate the slack in the schedule for each activity as the difference between its early and late finishes. *Total slack* is the amount of time an activity can be delayed beyond its earliest possible completion time without delaying the project's completion beyond its deadline. Activities on a path share the total slack.

Free slack is the amount of time an activity can be delayed beyond its earliest possible completion without delaying the start of any other activity in the network.

Now forget about the slack in the schedule! As a project manager, I keep my eye on it, but I usually leave it out of project reports and communications.

CPM Example

Table 10-2 takes our simple example from Table 10-1 and extends it to include estimated durations. From this information, we can develop a network diagram, such as the one depicted in Figure 10-3.

To develop a schedule for this project, we apply the CPM algorithm, beginning with the forward pass. Since the earliest possible start of an activity is the latest of its predecessors' earliest possible finishes, activity D cannot start until after activity B is finished. Accordingly, even though the early finish for activity A is day 4, activity E has to start after activity D is finished at day 12.

Next, we perform the backward pass. We will assume that the target deadline for the project is day 20. For each activity, the latest possible finish of an activity is the earliest of its successors' latest possible starts. Activities A, D, and F all have two successors, and their late finishes are set accordingly.

Table 10-2 A Critical Path Method (CPM) Example

Activity	Successor(s)	Duration
A	B, E	4
B	D	3
C	D	2
D	E, F	5
E	G	3
F	G, H	4
G	None	2
H	None	3

Figure 10-3   CPM Network Schedule Example

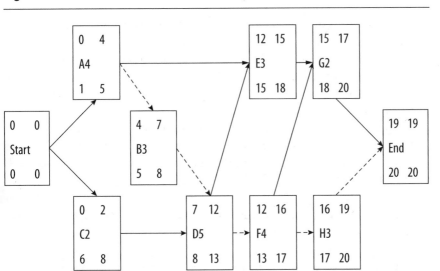

Identifying the critical path(s), we can see that A-B-D-F-H spans from the project's start to its finish, with an overall duration of 19 days.

Remember that to evaluate the slack in the schedule, look at the difference between each activity's early and late finishes. The critical path(s) will have the least amount of slack in the network—in this case, one day. Activities on a path with slack share the total slack. In this example, we can see that activities E and G have a total slack of three days. Free slack is illustrated by activity C, with six days of slack.

Note the similarities between the idea of a critical path and the theory of constraints (see Chapter 7). Any delay on a critical path will delay the overall project. In the same way, any problem with a bottleneck resource will make the whole process take longer (thereby reducing throughput, or project completion).

All of this analysis is easily done by hand. The mental walk-through of the network is invaluable in creating a common understanding of interdependencies among the project team. On an ongoing basis, however, it is advisable to have a computerized system for updating the schedule and tracking project status.

Project Management Software Systems

There is a plethora of *project management software systems* (*PMSSs*) that can be used to build the network model and project schedule. Some of the tools are stand-alone, workstation-based packages. They tend to be the simplest to learn but also the least powerful in complex analyses. They are really personal productivity tools for the project manager to use in tracking and reporting project progress.

One commonly used report is a *Gantt* chart, developed by engineer and management scientist Henry Gantt, which was initially used for large infrastructure projects such as the Hoover Dam in the first half of the 20th century (see http://ganttchart.com). This graphical representation focuses on the dimension of time and indicates the general timing and sequence of activities using bars that represent activity durations. A PMSS makes it easy to develop Gantt charts, although their usefulness declines as the complexity of a project increases.

Other PMSSs are developed for use over local area networks, either as separate packages or as module in an enterprise resource planning (ERP) system, and they usually cost much more money. This approach lets the entire project team access the project plan and make updates. Networked systems are more complex to learn, use, and manage, at least initially. If you will be able to use it repeatedly for different projects, then the initial investment of time and money may be worthwhile.

Remember that you might lose some of the collective view of the project and the team members' engagement if you skip developing the network as a group exercise—or try to conduct it electronically. Yes, you can project the software screen for everyone to see, but you may lose people's attention as they focus on different parts of the screen or have difficulty following what is being entered into the system. I recommend developing the network model and schedule on paper as a team and then entering the information into a PMSS—along with all the other information you will need to manage the project such as budget, resource assignments, and responsibilities—for ongoing reporting and control later.

In the next chapter, we will address managing a project from schedule to completion. For now, suffice it to say that there are benefits to a networked schedule:

- You know your true schedule.
- You know where you can/must compress the schedule.

- You know where you can "level," or smooth out resource demands to minimize the total amount needed at any one point in time.
- You know the impact of schedule changes.

Application and Reflection

1. If you saw a project plan that had an activity called "final report," what would you take that to mean? Is it to draft the report, edit it, circulate it for approval, copy it? This reinforces the importance of verbs in the WBS, so it is clear what has to be done.
2. Think about a project you need to tackle. What major chunks can you break it into? Would you define the work packages in phases or deliverables?

SUMMARY

Work breakdown structures identify the specific activities to be performed on a project by progressively dividing the project into smaller, more manageable pieces—work packages composed of activities. Work packages are typically defined in terms of deliverables or project phases.

Network models provide a logical representation of the project plan, capturing the dependencies and duration of each activity. Comprising nodes and arrows, network models can incorporate an extensive amount of information about a project. Typically, a network model is used to develop a project schedule.

In the activity-on-node network model, nodes contain activity information and arrows indicate logical dependencies. All nodes, except the Start and Finish nodes, must have at least one predecessor and one successor. All nodes except milestones have nonzero durations. Task durations are estimated in elapsed working time, and the information is added to the appropriate node.

The critical path method algorithm starts with the forward pass, which determines the earliest the activities and project can be finished. The backward pass starts at the project deadline and considers the latest point at which each activity can start and finish without delaying the overall project. Early and late start and finish times should also be recorded on the node.

The difference between an activity's early finish and late finish is that activity's slack. Activities on a branch of a network share the total slack. Free slack is specific to an individual activity.

The critical path is the path of longest duration (and therefore the one with the least amount of slack). A network may have multiple critical paths at one time. The critical path can change as the project progresses and the schedule is updated. The critical path of a project can be viewed as a bottleneck in a process. It determines the overall rate of completion.

Review Questions

1. In a WBS, activities are subdivided into work packages that can be uniquely assigned.
   a. True
   b. False
2. Which of the following is *not* an acceptable form for a work package?
   a. Departments
   b. Phases
   c. Deliverables
   d. All of the above are acceptable forms of work packages.
3. A network model contains which of the following?
   a. Nodes
   b. Arrows
   c. Logic
   d. a and b
   e. All of the above
4. Which of the following statements about network models for project management is *false*?
   a. Milestones have zero duration.
   b. Nodes can only represent activities.
   c. There can be only one starting point.
   d. Logic drives the project schedule.
5. When estimating task durations for a project plan, you should _____.
   a. indicate how much time you will spend on the task
   b. use a "best case," or optimistic, estimate of the duration
   c. plan to use elapsed time from a task's start to completion
   d. a and c
   e. All of the above

6. When conducting the _____ using the critical path method, you determine the late start and finish times for each activity.
   a. forward pass
   b. backward pass
   c. slack analysis
   d. critical path evaluation
7. The critical path is defined as _____.
   a. the most important activities
   b. the path of longest duration
   c. the activities with the least amount of slack
   d. b and c
   e. All of the above
8. How does the theory of constraints explain the critical path method?
   a. By emphasizing that the goal to make money should be a primary objective
   b. By relating the critical path to a bottleneck that determines the rate of throughput
   c. By distinguishing between free and total slack in terms of throughput
   d. By allowing SON, FNLT, and SNET constraints to be used in activity definitions
9. A Gantt chart is useful for _____.
   a. communicating project status
   b. controlling project costs
   c. evaluating free and total slack
   d. measuring project quality
10. PMSSs are useful for _____.
   a. helping the project team develop the WBS
   b. ensuring the quality of project deliverables
   c. determining what information the stakeholders should receive
   d. updating the project with changes to status

11

PROJECT CONTROL

Two are better than one, because they have a good return for their work.

—ECCLESIASTES 4:9

arlier in the book, we talked about the Pareto principle (also known as the 80/20 rule) in the context of quality management: 80 percent of quality problems typically arise from 20 percent of the possible causes. I believe that the Pareto principle applies in another way: 80 percent of the work in project management—that is, defining the project, breaking down the work, developing the network, and evaluating the schedule—yields 20 percent of the benefit. Subsequently, especially for complex projects, 80 percent of the benefit of formal project management comes from the remaining 20 percent of the effort, or project control. There are some basic things you can do to keep a project on track.

After completing this chapter, you should be able to do the following:

- Apply the *project control* process
- Perform project *cost analysis*

- Describe project control problems
- Close or *terminate* a project effectively
- Identify contributing factors for a productive project team
- Conduct an effective meeting

PROJECT CONTROL

Project control might better be called "project navigation," the way in which the project is steered and the current position assessed over the course of the project. Although you may have done a thorough job of planning and scheduling the work, things rarely go as planned. However, by comparing where you are in a project to where you want to be at a particular point, you can address issues in a timely manner.

For example, I worked with an organization that was going through an accreditation process similar to ISO certification. Much of the focus of the project was on establishing consistent processes, allowing for continuous improvement, establishing outcome measures, and documenting all of it. Working with the various people assigned to the project, I had developed a *timeline* that reflected interdependencies and allowed for necessary approvals and potential adjustments.

We used this plan as the basis for our monthly status meetings. Had we finished what we were supposed to finish? Had we started what was supposed to be started? Updating the schedule with actual start and finish dates gave the project team and sponsor a clear view of the project's progress. Unfortunately, after five months, it was clear that the team would not be able to finish the requisite tasks by the overall deadline.

As a result, the project sponsor agreed to a different, albeit more expensive, approach that would get the work done in a quality manner on a timely basis. The project ended as a success and became a benchmark for other organizations pursuing similar accreditation.[1]

Effective project control also enables project leaders to manage how and when other types of changes occur. At the onset, the project sponsor and project manager should determine the process for discussing and approving substantive changes to the project's scope and schedule. This is crucial to managing expectations and overall project success.

It is common in information systems development projects for the scope of a system to change with the addition of data elements, reports, features, and so on. When that happens, it is important to identify the work to be done and assess its impact on the schedule for the current scope. Often, such scope creep requests will be deferred, and the enhancement will be made in a subsequent update to the system. If the change is agreed to (or mandated), then the project manager should revise the statement of work, project schedule, and budget accordingly, then clearly communicate the impact of the change to the team, the sponsor, and the stakeholders.

Another aspect of change management is the need to mitigate the impact of project progression on other parts of the organization. Information systems projects also illustrate this need. When implementing a new transaction-based system, it is important to conduct "stress tests" to ensure that the system will operate properly at peak volume. It is likely that this will require a change in the typical processing schedule for a data center; this is coordinated with the system manager so as not to disrupt operations or response times for other transaction processing.

At the core of all these project control concerns is the need for clear, credible, and consistent *communication*. This is essential within the project team, but it is also important to address with project stakeholders. It is a good idea to have a communications plan that identifies who should receive what information, how often, and in what format.

There can be a wide range of communication needs. You might update an executive team only at key milestones, focusing on costs and deliverables. Some projects merit meeting daily with key members of the project team to coordinate resources. Regardless, the cardinal rule is to keep the project sponsor well informed; you do not want him or her to be surprised with news about the project from someone else!

Typically, I use a simple approach for providing updates on project status to people outside the project team. I capture accomplishments, plans, and issues for the reporting period on one sheet of paper. If the stakeholder I am briefing is concerned with budget matters, I attach a cost analysis, as shown in the next section of this chapter. Note that this information is gained through the project control process.

Sample Project Update Format

Here is an example of a typical project update (it extends the example of the silent auction begun in Chapter 9):

VOCATIONAL SERVICES GALA SILENT AUCTION

Project Status Update
As of September 20th

Accomplishments to Date
- Recruited ace team of solicitors
- Assigned solicitation responsibilities:
  - Bob—sports memorabilia and athletic experiences
  - Barb—art and home decor
  - Allison—children's items and family experiences
  - Ivey—last year's donors
  - Linda—all other
- Finalized the solicitation paperwork: ask letter and donation form
- Started collecting merchandising items (baskets, boxes for risers)
- Have commitments for: one week on the Mexican Riviera, a long weekend in North Myrtle Beach, one closet organized, one sales account plan, one project plan, conductor for a song at a concert performed by the local symphony, one door awning, a one-hour massage

Plans for the Next Two Weeks
- Meet with Allison to get her started (Ivey)
- Begin actively soliciting prospects (all)
- Set up auction database on the Web for shared access (Ivey)
- Ask for Vocational Services–specific donations, such as a dinner for eight prepared by chef at home (Linda)
- Check on consignment options (Linda)
- Conduct a checkpoint meeting to assess and adjust (all)

Concerns and Questions
- Is Jim available to solicit auction items with Bob?
- Can we ask each Vocational employee for a donation or solicitation (hairdresser, nail technician, and so on)? We would like to stress 100 percent participation.
- Barbara needs the names of any contacts for decorators, art gallery owners, and so on.

Project Control Process

The underlying process for project control defines who will update the activity status, the frequency for updating the plan routinely, and the manner of disseminating information among the team members. You might want to meet with the team weekly and note the updates then. Alternatively, you might want certain individuals or team members to update the project status daily using a shared project management software system.

When I worked in the Olympic management operations project office for a worldwide Olympic sponsor, our practice was to collect the updates in writing, update the schedule in the PMSS, and use revised reports as the basis for discussion in biweekly meetings. This saved us from having to train everyone on using the PMSS, which would have been used only by this one project team, whose members would disperse after the Olympics.

As mentioned in Chapter 10, any PMSS will allow you to capture scads of data on each activity in a project (remember how useful nodes are in a network diagram?). You can track resource utilization, cost centers, budget allocations, and more. Maintaining data is costly, so you want to update only the information that you really need to control the project.

For project control, what you truly want to manage is time. It is the easiest and most concrete metric for tracking project status. Time also determines your ability to meet cost and quality targets. These three dimensions of project performance are interrelated; for example, less time often means higher costs and lower quality.

The relationships are dynamic. A change in one dimension causes changes in the other two. If the required scope/quality is increased, then you can expect the project to take longer and become more costly. On the other hand, if you saved some time on a work package, that will probably also save you money, enable you to add to the quality, or both. The relationship is not mathematically geometric; the point is to emphasize the interdependent nature of the success factors.

So, as you work on updating the project plan, focus on the time. When an activity has been started, record the actual start date. When an activity is finished, note the actual finish date. I strongly advise against using percent complete, at least for schedule control. The effort and difficulty of a task are not necessarily uniform as the task is executed. So saying something is 80 percent done does not really tell you anything (other than it is not finished). If you need to, you can change the duration to reflect changes in expectations of completion dates. This makes your schedule more valid and gives your project team a results-oriented outlook.

As I write this, I am reminded of my experience of having a house built. The cabinetmaker told me the cabinets were "90 percent done" well after we had moved in. (He is a terrific person, and the cabinets are beautiful.) My point is that perceptions of percent complete are very subjective. I have only found this element useful for budget allocation and tracking, and even then, I prefer the approach discussed in the following section.

Cost Control

Cost control is concerned with influencing the factors that create changes, determining whether the cost baseline has changed, and managing the actual changes as they occur. As with project (schedule) control, cost control enables the project manager to do several things:

- Monitor to detect variances from the plan
- Ensure that changes are recorded correctly
- Prevent inappropriate changes from being made
- Inform stakeholders of authorized changes

Project clients and sponsors tend to be more interested in cost analyses than in schedule updates. As a project manager, you should manage internal team reporting based on time but be prepared to perform the following cost analyses:

Budgeted cost of work performed (BCWP)
Actual cost of work performed (ACWP)
Budgeted cost of work scheduled (BCWS)
Estimate to completion (ETC)
Estimate at completion (EAC)

What you are doing is comparing actual results to plans at different times during the project's progression. Think of BCWS as the *baseline*; if the project is proceeding according to plan, this number reflects how much money has been spent up to a certain point in time (t). It reflects what you and the team expected when you first developed the project plan. At time t, you should have accomplished a target amount of work (the work scheduled) and spent a target amount of money (the budget).

When you compare BCWS with BCWP, you are analyzing the *schedule variance* (SV), which is equal to BCWP − BCWS. If the schedule variance is negative (the work performed is less than the work scheduled), you are obviously behind schedule. Comparing BCWP with ACWP provides the *cost variance* (CV). If ACWP − BCWP is positive, this indicates that your project is over budget, since you have actually spent more than you budgeted for the work performed to date. Different combinations of these variances are shown graphically in Figure 11-1.

Earlier, I eschewed the use of percent complete as a measure for project control. It can, however, be useful for project communication, specifically in the calculation of earned value, a single number that indicates project progress. *Earned value* is the sum of percent complete multiplied by the BCWP for all the activities in the project: Σ [percent complete of activity i $\times$ BCWP$_i$] for all activities, $i = 1$ to N. This is an approximation not a valid analysis, because it is based on percent complete, so do not use it to control your project. It is reasonable, however, to report it to stakeholders as a rough indicator of progress.

Since percent complete is a specious number, there are numerous ways to estimate progress on a task. One is known as "50-50": you mark the task as 50 percent complete when it is started, then add the other 50 percent when

Figure 11-1 Graphical Depiction of Variance Analysis

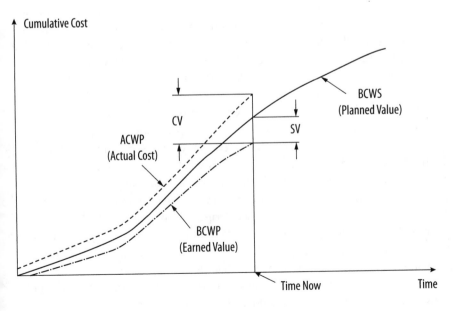

it is completed. Another convention is using "100 percent complete" when the task is complete and "0 complete" before that. A common heuristic is estimating the percentage of completion by using the percentage of cost expended to the total cost budgeted for a task.[2]

You can see that the approach I favor is reflected in the second option described. It is arguably the most conservative estimate of the three. Whatever heuristic you use, remember that estimates should not be taken as measures of reality.

Another number in which project stakeholders will be interested is the estimate at completion (EAC). Based on where the project is now, how much is it likely to cost when it is done? To calculate this, you need to have an idea of whether the current variance will continue or whether you want to hold to your budget for the remaining work to be done. This determines your estimate to completion (ETC). Then your EAC = ETC + ACWP.

For example, assume that analysis of your project's status indicates that the ratio of BCWP to ACWP is x percent. Do you want to project that your remaining work will also cost x percent of the budgeted amount? Again, I favor a conservative approach, so even if $x < 1$ and the project is under budget, I might not change my ETC at time t. The overall EAC_t will still be less than the original BCWP ($BCWP_0$), reflecting the positive variance to date. On the other hand, if $x \geq 1$, a conservative approach would be to revise the formula to $EAC_t = x \times BCWP_0$.

The way you determine the EAC is arguably more political than mathematical. Is it better to underrate positive variances so the project sponsor will be pleasantly surprised with performance that is better than expected at the end of the project? Is it better to deliver bad news in small increments, or will a negative variance be overlooked in light of a completed project? As we have established, customer satisfaction depends on how well the customer thinks the project's results meet expectations. In addition to the SOW, the EAC is another important way to manage expectations.

Technically, your ETC will depend on your assessment of risk factors, how far along you are in the project, and whether the variances experienced to date have been anomalies. Costs can escalate for many reasons. The budget might be based on guesswork. You might have to replace a key resource or use a different approach than you originally planned. A technology may be underperforming. The learning curve might be steeper than anticipated. Environmental factors beyond the project team's control, such as political or economic conditions, can also contribute to cost escalation.

Poor project management may also be to blame. Perhaps the initial plan was erroneous, work is being done inefficiently, morale is bad, or communications are unclear. Project control might be weak. Problems with project control often arise in these situations:

- There is a change in key players that undermines the organization's commitment to the project.
- The organizational culture resists the discipline of the control process.
- The information you are receiving from project team members is inaccurate (overly optimistic or otherwise biased).

As the project leader, you should have insight into what has caused any cost escalation. You may also be in a position to correct or mitigate it. In any case, the revised estimate at time t is $EAC_t = ACWP_t + ETC_t$.

PROJECT CLOSINGS

Closing a project is a process that is often neglected. We are quick to move on to other things. High-performance operations invest the time necessary to capture the knowledge gained from the project. Organizational learning contributes to continuous improvement.

As with project planning, *project closings* can range in formality. Your organization may have detailed requirements for how project materials must be archived. At a minimum, I like to have a postmortem meeting to discuss the project's conduct. In terms of documentation, I recommend a "postcompletion project summary." This is a one- or two-page document that captures how things went differently than expected, for better or worse, and has recommendations for future improvements. A sample format is presented in Figure 11-2.

A postmortem analysis is helpful whether the project has been run smoothly to completion or not. A project might be terminated midcourse. Sometimes projects fail. As the following list suggests, these are remarkable opportunities to learn from experience and avert such pitfalls in the future.

Patterns of Contributing Causes to Failure[3]
Ignore the project environment.
Push a new technology to market too quickly.
Don't bother building in fallback options.
When problems occur, shoot the most visible.
Let new ideas starve to death through inertia.
Don't bother conducting feasibility studies.

Never admit a project is a failure.
Overmanage your project managers and their teams.
Never, never conduct postfailure reviews.
Never bother to understand project trade-offs.
Allow political expediency and infighting to dictate important project decisions.
Make sure the project is run by a weak leader.

While somewhat tongue-in-cheek, these admonitions highlight the key ways a project's likelihood of success can be undermined.

Figure 11-2   Post-Completion Project Review Protocol

GENERAL PROJECT INFORMATION

Project #		Project Name	
Closing Date		Review Date	
Project Manager		Review Leader	

ACCOMPLISHMENTS
Consider the following questions:

What were the technical points of interest in this project?

Did we advance professional practice in some way?

How did we meet the project's objectives?

Did we exceed the clients' expectations? In what ways?

Is there marketing potential in the results of this project?

Did we develop or leverage a new capability in the firm?

How might we build on these accomplishments?

FINDINGS:

_____

_____

_____

_____

_____

LEARNINGS

Consider the following questions:

What were the surprises in the project?

What went differently than was planned? (Consider scope, costs, schedule, deliverables, risks, communications, and results.)

What issues, if any, did the sponsor have with the project?

Did we have the right people involved in the work?

Were external resources needed for the project? Should these capabilities be developed in-house, for future projects?

What might have been done differently?

FINDINGS:

_____

_____

_____

_____

_____

Project Terminations

A project may be terminated, or ended before it is completed, because the original plan is no longer valid. This may mean that the objectives have been met in some other way or perhaps that environmental factors have changed so that the realizable benefits are no longer acceptable. Termination can be abrupt or gradual. Ideally, you still want to perform a postmortem to understand what happened and whether things might have gone differently. Retrospective reflection can improve future projections.

The idea of "termination" seems negative and may take some bravery to face. Despite the old adage "Don't throw good money after bad," it is hard to acknowledge that a project that is under way cannot succeed. Many people view *termination* as synonymous with *failure*. In reality, though, a project fails when it is completed and does not meet its objective.

Project Failures

At the onset of a project, you define success in your SOW in terms of a primary objective. This dimension of success reflects the impact of the project. You may have been an outstanding project manager and delivered what was asked for when it was needed and within budget. But if the deliverable does not have the desired impact, then the project is a failure.

Conversely, you may be late and over budget, but if the result wildly exceeds expectations, then you have succeeded. The interstate highway system in the United States, referred to as the Eisenhower highway system, was such a case:

> President Eisenhower sold the American people on the interstate system largely because of its benefits to national defense: fast, modern highways would help the United States fight and then recover from a nuclear war. Four decades later, that expectation seems pretty quaint, and nowhere near as compelling as the highway system's benefits in terms of safety, economic development, and enhancement of national commerce.[4]

You might remember that success or failure goes beyond the dimensions of time, cost, and quality to include politics.

The politics of perception can go awry because of bad timing, inaccurate stakeholder assessments, or a poor reputation in general. An example of bad timing is renovating offices (on time, within budget, and in good taste) when people are being laid off. To illustrate misperceptions of stakeholders, consider the Hubble telescope, a well-executed project with remarkable scientific achievements. Ask most taxpayers about it, though, and they recall that the mirrors were not adjusted properly and the telescope initially provided blurry images. It is important to manage perceptions (pun intended).

EFFECTIVE PROJECT TEAMS

Another consideration in project control is project team relationships. Low morale, uncooperative members, and ineffective conflict resolution can all undermine how the project is conducted and its ultimate success. Of course, it helps to have competent members and committed project sponsors. These are necessary but not sufficient requirements for effective project teams. It is important for the project leader to set the tone and manage the personalities on the team.

Many problems can be averted with collaborative project planning. Whenever possible, include the members of your project teams in the development of the statement of work, work breakdown structure, and project schedule. The more involved people are at the onset, the more they understand what is to be done and how to go about it; as the opening quote suggests, two participants are better than one.

If you do not have the luxury of a fully staffed project in the beginning, take the time to indoctrinate new team members as they are added. Make sure they are clear about roles and responsibilities. Appoint mentors to help inexperienced team members develop necessary relationships and understand operating policies. Work to achieve a collaborative climate based on mutual trust and respect.

Productive teamwork results when the goals are clear and members understand how their activities are to be coordinated. That is why project management is such an effective way to achieve results: the goals are specified, and the interrelationships are identified. Communications are also intentional, specific, and regular with sound project control, ensuring that team members understand the project's status and the implications of any changes.

TECHNIQUE: CONDUCTING EFFECTIVE MEETINGS

Whether we are talking about new product development, implementation of new technology, or process improvement projects, most aspects of operations management require *meetings*. I find it ironic that one of the biggest wastes of time I have experienced in business is poorly run meetings, even though the meetings are ostensibly to improve operational quality and efficiency.

We could probably all come up with a "Top Ten" list of reasons why meetings can be such a waste of time. Here is mine:

10. The wrong people are in the meeting.
9. Participants do not give the meeting their full attention; they are distracted by side conversations or electronic interruptions.
8. One person inappropriately dominates the conversation.
7. Participants are passive observers and do not contribute.
6. The discussion gets bogged down in tangential issues that cannot be solved in this meeting with this group of people.
5. The meeting does not start on time.
4. People arrive late, either missing what has already been discussed or causing the others to repeat themselves.
3. The meeting is unnecessary.
2. The meeting lacks a clear purpose and agenda.
1. Participants are unprepared for their role in the meeting.

As we rely on technology and video teleconferencing for more and more meetings, these issues are exacerbated with additional distractions.

It would seem to be common sense to have a clear idea of what has to be accomplished in a meeting, who needs to be there, and what they need to do in advance to be prepared. So why doesn't common sense prevail? I suggest laziness and busyness are to blame for the lack of meaningful preparation and sloppy conduct. Over the long term, low expectations become ingrained in the organizational culture.

Preparation to Consider Before the Meeting

While you and I may not be able to correct all the meetings in the world, there are things we can do to run effective meetings and, in the context of project control, establish a culture of excellence and high expectations. I suggest that before you call a meeting, you ask yourself some basic questions:

- **What is the purpose of the meeting?** There are many different types of meetings—task-oriented work sessions, problem-solving gatherings, creative meetings, communications assemblies, policy definition summits, and so on. Understanding the purpose informs the agenda, participants, and preparation needed.[5]

- **Is a meeting the best way to accomplish this purpose?** For example, a status update might take you an hour to prepare and take the others five minutes to read—possibly saving hours of time on their part. Social networking using electronic collaboration tools might be a better way to report progress or solve a problem.

- **How should the meeting proceed?** Prepare an agenda that specifies the purpose and the process for the meeting. If different people are responsible for leading different portions of the meeting, note their names. If possible, allocate time estimates for each agenda item.

- **Whose participation is crucial? Who would be nice to have but not indispensible for the meeting?** Schedule the meeting around the availability of the key participants, not everyone. If some people complain, assure them that you will send out a meeting summary, so they will know what was discussed.

- **What preparations do others need to make for the meeting to be effective?** When you distribute the agenda, be clear about your expectations for participants' preparation. You may want to brief an executive in a premeeting meeting to ensure his or her readiness. Others may warrant a follow-up phone call: "Just checking to make sure you have what you need for our meeting." Over time, this diligence will create a climate of accountability that will be appreciated by most of your colleagues.

- **What do you need to prepare to make the meeting successful?** In addition to the work you have done to address the preceding questions, give some thought to how the meeting environment should be arranged to encourage participants' engagement in the discussion. Another key decision is whether or not specific roles should be assigned within the meeting. Meeting roles include chairperson, *facilitator*, scribe, timekeeper, and issue tracker.

You may feel that you can perform all these roles. I find it politic to have someone who tends to be verbose be the timekeeper. Someone who is likely to have his or her own agenda (such as wanting to focus on a side issue) is a good issue tracker. It is important to have good notes from the meeting because you should distribute a summary to everyone involved afterward, so I often have a scribe (whose notes supplement mine). You, as the chairperson, can also be the facilitator in most types of meetings. It is important to have someone who can maintain an open and balanced conversational flow.[6] If I am very invested in the outcome of the meeting or want to contribute ideas but don't want to seem like I have already decided the answer, I'll ask someone from outside the project to be a facilitator. The most important thing is to be able to maintain a common focus during the meeting.

Another aspect of preparation is whether ground rules should be established at the start of the meeting. Is this a group of people who are comfortable with a free flow of discussion? I sometimes find it helpful to use an icebreaker to get a meeting going. For example, brainstorming 25 uses for a pencil gives you a good opportunity to remind people of a few basics:

- Build on each other's ideas
- Reserve judgment
- Have only one person speak at a time
- Obey the facilitator

You might also have some key individuals who will not speak out in the meeting. They may be painfully shy. They may not trust others in the meeting. Or they may be self-conscious about speaking if their supervisors are in the room. You have several options for dealing with them. Sometimes, if you call on them, the invitation to speak gives them the license they feel they need. In other cases, you might want to catch them before the meeting to get their input and then just speak on their behalf, giving credit where credit is due. Over time, you will learn what works best for your team members.

Action to Take During and After the Meeting

Try to stick to the *agenda*, as long as it serves the purpose of the meeting. Be respectful of others' ideas and time. Do not let the meeting run late. If an issue arises, capture it on paper and commit to addressing it in another forum, as appropriate. Spend at least the last few minutes on next steps, which should include people and time frames. Thank everyone for their participation and acknowledge contributions.

When you are trying to establish group norms, it is occasionally helpful to give everyone a chance to read off the same page—literally. You might find it useful to distribute a reading assignment before a big meeting or planning session or at the close of the preceding meeting to encourage people to reflect on desired behaviors. While it is likely that some participants will not read the assigned material, you might still achieve a critical mass of team members who understand and support the norms, improving the overall performance of the team.

For working through teamwork issues, I favor John Maxwell's *The 17 Indisputable Laws of Teamwork Workbook.* You might take time at regular meetings to tackle one law at a time—or have an off-site team-building session organized around the entire list. To apply humor to and raise awareness about problems with the team culture, another good resource is Patrick Lencioni's *The Five Dysfunctions of a Team: A Leadership Fable.* It is a quick read, and by focusing on another team's issues, it makes the situation less threatening.

When you schedule the meeting, schedule some time for yourself afterward, if you can. I find that some people will want to share a thought privately after the meeting, so I stick around after the session, ostensibly straightening up and organizing my notes. Also, use that time to craft a meeting summary before the ink on your notes has dried. The sooner you do it, the less time it will take.

Meeting summaries provide several important functions. They serve as a group memory, which helps to avoid rehashing old decisions. You can disseminate information to interested parties who did not attend the meeting. Summaries also provide a measure of quality control, ensuring a common understanding of what was discussed and decided. I find that they also contribute to the culture of accountability and engagement.

Action to Take if It Isn't Your Meeting

Early in my career, I went to any and every meeting I could. I wanted to learn about the organization, the people involved, and the projects. And my time was not incredibly valuable in those early days.

At some point, though, a professional wants to become more discriminating in the use of his or her time. This is especially true in the age of electronic calendars and automated meeting invitations. Before you agree to participate, make sure that you investigate a bit:

- Ask for the purpose, the agenda, and the participants list. It does not hurt to ask, especially when you couch it in terms such as "so I can be prepared."
- Know what *you* want to accomplish in the session.

For example, I might go to a meeting to create an opportunity for an informal discussion with participants before or afterward to get some help on a project or an issue I am working on. Your goal may be to influence the outcome of the meeting or provide an important perspective. The idea is to be intentional about how you spend your time. We will delve into this topic more deeply in the next chapter.

Application and Reflection

1. Consider a completed project that you were involved in, either as a team member or the project leader. On your own, conduct a post-mortem to see what key lessons you should have learned.
2. Evaluate a meeting you recently attended. Were any of the "Top Ten" reasons for an ineffective meeting evident? What would you have done differently if you had been the person who called the meeting?

SUMMARY

Project control is a critical success factor for a project's successful completion. It should be performed as a routine, regularly scheduled process to update project status, adjust the project plan, and communicate progress as needed. Following a consistent control process makes it easier to share timely information and receive an early warning of issues.

To report on project costs, it is necessary to determine how much work has been performed on an activity-by-activity basis. Percent complete is imprecise and subjective, but there are alternative ways to estimate progress on a task. In one known as 50-50, you mark the task as 50 percent complete when it is started, then add the other 50 percent when it is completed. Another convention is to use "100 percent complete" when the task is complete and "0 complete" before that.

Project cost analysis compares the actual cost of work performed to the budgeted cost of work performed. Comparing the budgeted cost of work scheduled to the budgeted cost of work performed indicates whether there is a schedule variance. The estimate at completion is likely to change as the project progresses. Typically, a projection is made based on the percentage of budgeted cost to the actual cost for the work performed to date.

Project control issues can surface for a variety of reasons: poor planning, inefficient processes, bad morale, unclear communications, and weak control. Control can be undermined when there is a change in key players and/or the commitment to the project, the organizational culture resists the discipline of the control process, or the information the project manager receives from team members is inaccurate.

High-performing organizations take the time to conduct orderly project closings. At a minimum, this should involve a documented postmortem meeting with key players to compare plans and assumptions to actual results and identify opportunities for further improvement in project planning. Many lessons can be learned from project failures and terminations.

Productive teamwork results when goals are clear and members understand how their activities should be coordinated. Ongoing team communications are intentional, specific, and routine, ensuring that the team members understand the project's status and the implications of any changes.

Effective meetings result from a clear idea of what has to be accomplished in the meeting, who needs to be there, and what they need to do in advance to be prepared. Preparation of an agenda and distribution of meeting summaries are essential to creating a culture of accountability and accomplishment.

Review Questions

1. Which of the following statements about project control is *false?*
   a. It helps to address issues in a timely manner.
   b. It involves assessing the current status of a project.
   c. It is dependent on how the SOW is organized.
   d. It helps to determine if and when changes are needed.
2. When the scope of an information systems development project changes, _____.
   a. the SOW should be changed
   b. the project manager should be changed
   c. the schedule and budget estimates should be changed
   d. a and c
   e. All of the above

3. The project control process should _____.
    a. be performed on a regular basis
    b. provide status updates
    c. identify issues and concerns
    d. b and c
    e. All of the above

4. To determine whether your project is under or over budget, you should evaluate _____.
    a. ACWP — BCWP
    b. BCWP — BCWS
    c. BCWS — BCWP
    d. ACWP/BCWP

5. To determine whether your project is ahead or behind schedule, you should evaluate _____.
    a. ACWP — BCWP
    b. BCWP — BCWS
    c. BCWS — BCWP
    d. ACWP/BCWP

6. The ETC should consider _____.
    a. BCWP/ACWP
    b. risk factors
    c. anomalies
    d. b and c
    e. All of the above

7. Which of the following is *not* a typical reason for cost escalation?
    a. The learning curve is inadequate.
    b. The project was poorly planned.
    c. Project control is weak.
    d. The approach has changed.

8. When should a project postmortem be done?
    a. The project has failed.
    b. The project is terminated.
    c. The project is completed.
    d. a and b
    e. All of the above

9. Productive teamwork results when the goals are clear, members understand how their activities should be coordinated, and people are closely supervised.
    a. True
    b. False

10. **Which of the following does *not* contribute to effective meetings?**
    a. Discussing issues until everyone is satisfied
    b. Distributing a meeting agenda before the meeting
    c. Relying on videoconferencing technology
    d. Distinguishing between essential and optional participants

12

INDIVIDUAL EFFECTIVENESS

A chain is no stronger than its weakest link.
—ENGLISH PROVERB

S omething that often amazes me is how well management theory applies to individuals as well as to organizations. You can view yourself as a system, establish performance metrics, and strive for continuous improvement. In this chapter, I strive to provide a synthesis of everything we have covered in this book with an illustration of how key concepts can be applied to improve your individual effectiveness.

After completing this chapter, you should be able to do the following:

- Draw parallels between organizational performance and *individual effectiveness*
- Apply key operations management concepts to develop individual improvement plans
- Improve your *personal effectiveness* in the workplace

Your personal effectiveness is critical to your success. I believe that for operations to be managed effectively, processes and projects must be performed effectively. For processes and projects to be managed effectively, individuals (particularly managers) must perform effectively. This reflects a hierarchy of prepotency in operations management—lower levels in the hierarchy must be accomplished before higher levels can be achieved, as shown in Figure 12-1.

This suggests that to run a well-managed project, a project manager should be organized and personally effective; otherwise, the project will become disorganized and likely fail. If a process has been identified for a Six Sigma improvement, the project has to be well managed or change will not be achieved, or if it is achieved, it will be more costly than intended. If an organization does not emphasize the need for quality processes, it is unlikely to achieve the desired results.

YOU AS AN OPERATIONAL SYSTEM

Operations are a critical success factor for most organizations and can be a key element in a company's competitive advantage. Similarly, the ways in which you operate are central to your individual effectiveness.

Figure 12-1   Performance Hierarchy

Adding Value

Viewing the individual as an operational system provides several insights, particularly regarding job performance. For example, think of yourself as a transformation function that adds value to inputs to create outputs, and consider how you add value in the organization. Is the amount of time you spend on non-value-adding activities significant? If so, how can you reduce or eliminate them from your work?

Applying systems thinking can provide further ideas to improve individual effectiveness. Recall that organizational systems tend to have numerous feedback loops and permeable boundaries with the environment (factors outside the system's control). You might ask yourself if you have accurate and timely feedback loops. For example, reviewing your completion rates on a weekly "to accomplish" list might help you to be more realistic in your commitments. If not, take steps to establish them.

One way to look at an individual's boundaries and environment are to distinguish between a "circle of concern" and a "circle of influence."[1] The things that can affect your performance yet are out of your control are in your circle of concern. There should be some factors that you can mitigate; these are in your circle of influence. At a minimum, you should have a good understanding of where those boundaries lie. The closer the boundary of your influence is to that of your concern, the more effective you can be.

To increase your influence, consider how much initiative you take. Do you identify potential problems and thwart them, or do you react to issues as directed? If the latter is closer to the truth, then work on identifying problems proactively and presenting ideas to resolve them. You can also work on understanding what is in your circle of concern, being alert to changes and trends, and identifying ways to move those elements into your circle of influence.

Developing Capabilities

Applying a resource-based view to yourself can facilitate decisions to enhance or develop capabilities to raise your effectiveness and your opportunity set. This can be a difficult exercise, because you may overlook things that come easily to you, without realizing that they are rare capabilities.

Think of it as your personal development plan. In considering your capabilities, what can you do that is valuable, unusual, and usable? Are you prepared to leverage it to achieve your desired results?

INDIVIDUAL PERFORMANCE

Your performance will either contribute to or detract from the desired organizational performance. Individual effectiveness stems from three areas of focus: productive capacity, productivity, and quality. As with organizations, individuals benefit from developing goals with metrics to maintain balanced performance in each of these areas (see Chapter 3).

Protecting Productive Capacity

Productive capacity is really a throughput measure based on your health and sense of well-being. If you take care of yourself physically, emotionally, socially, and spiritually, you will be able to operate at your best.[2]

Conversely, if you are short on sleep and long on fast food, you will be more likely to make mistakes. Extended stretches of missing family dinners or lunch out with friends will add to your stress level instead of reducing it. Exercise, fresh air, and lots of drinking water are the best tools for preventive maintenance. Metrics for protecting personal productive capacity can include targets for time spent exercising, meditating, reading, being with family, and so on. Build that time into your schedule—studies have shown that predictable and scheduled time off from work improves individuals' professional productivity.[3]

Enhancing Individual Productivity

A key lever in organizational and process productivity is technology (see Chapter 6). Clearly, technology can be a black hole for time spent, whether because of endless social networking, unreliable performance, or steep learning curves. However, individuals who can leverage the potential access and immediacy technology provides arguably do more with less. By definition, this reflects increased productivity.

Are you using technology effectively? Are you skilled in the tools you use, particularly smart phones and personal digital assistants (PDAs)? Do you have backup copies of critical information for work and home? Do you subscribe to Web resources that are rich in information relevant to your work, or do you spend hours on the Internet browsing, chatting, linking, or otherwise surfing?

Information overload is one potential pitfall in the networked age. The theory of constraints tells us that in order to make money now and in the future, we must focus on throughput and cost reduction. In the context of the individual, costs are incurred by wasted time. Be intentional about how you establish e-mail filters, subscriptions, and update alerts. Set boundaries on the amount of time you spend on a technology if you find that it is a drain on your productivity. Set expectations of how soon you will respond to communications and be consistent (to avoid several follow-up messages). On average, knowledge workers change activities every three minutes, usually because they are distracted by an incoming communication.[4] You do not have to allow that to happen.

Of course, *time management* undergirds the challenges of leveraging technology and avoiding overload. Tips and tricks for time management abound. From years of study and practice, let me offer a synthesis of best practices that I have found to be useful:

- **Plan at the end of the day.** You will be more realistic about what you can accomplish.
- **Use a week-at-a-glance perspective.** Covey calls this a "helicopter view."[5] Planning day by day is too detailed and confining, and it tends to encourage overscheduling. When you can see that you have two hectic days in a row, you might be less inclined to commit to a half-day planning session on the third day. A week-at-a-glance helps you pace yourself.
- **Consider the dimension of energy as you plan along the time continuum.** The idea of energy can encompass clear thinking, positive attitude, and creativity, as well as physical vigor. You know there are times when you are at your best or at your worst, so plan accordingly. Perhaps you start the workweek raring to go—leverage that! Or perhaps you are drained by four in the afternoon; do not let yourself get embroiled in tough meetings at that time of day. Managing your energy makes better use of your time.
- **Projectize yourself.** "Transform everything into scintillating projects."[6] What that means is that you should look at the time you spend and identify things that are really projects. Make sure that each one has an explicit scope and clear objectives. Projectizing contributes to productivity in several ways. First, it may help you to realize that you have too many projects going at once. You probably perform several different roles at and outside of work. Considering all your roles and responsibilities can be enlightening. Sometimes a person will spend more time shifting between projects and less time working on them,

essentially creating a bottleneck. Concentrating on less may help you do more. Also, by thinking of your work as a project, you can focus on the desired results. It may also encourage you to break the work down into more manageable pieces. You may develop a better sense of what activities are critical and determine your overall rate of completion.

- **Perform *rolling wave planning*.** This means that you update your plans with specifics as time progresses. At the beginning of each month, look at the next forty days.[7] What specific things need to be accomplished as you consider all the different projects you have for each of your roles?

In Figure 12-2 you will see an example of an individual planning worksheet that can help you implement these suggestions. The weekly plan encourages making time for maintaining productivity capacity, or wellness. For each key role, you can specify what you want to accomplish and when during the week; for example, circulate a proposal draft, take Mom to lunch, make travel arrangements for an upcoming conference, and so on. The 40-day plan provides a longer-term perspective and facilitates spreading projects out more realistically.

Avoiding Waste

At a personal level, waste is the time, energy, or money you spend on something that is of no value to you. In Chapter 5, we identified seven types of waste in organizations. This list can help you evaluate the waste in your personal and professional life:

- **Overproduction:** Do you find yourself throwing food away?
- **Inventory:** Do you have too much stuff in your closets, drawers, and cabinets?
- **Waiting:** Can you do something you enjoy or find useful as you wait?
- **Unnecessary transport:** Do you find yourself backtracking, redoing work, or retracing your steps?
- **Unnecessary processing:** Is it necessary to respond to every message you receive?
- **Unnecessary human motions:** Are the things you use regularly easily accessible?
- **Defects:** Do you find yourself making mistakes when you are short on sleep?

Figure 12-2   Individual Planner

40-DAY PLAN—STARTING M/D/Y

WELLNESS IMPROVEMENT

Physical • Mental • Spiritual • Social

Milestones to be achieved

FAMILY RESPONSIBILITIES

Wife • Mother • Daughter • Sister • Niece

Milestones to be achieved

WORK ROLE 1

Project A • Project B • Project C

Milestones to be achieved

WORK ROLE 2

Project D • Project E • Project F

Milestones to be achieved

WORK ROLE 3

Project G • Project·H • Project J

Milestones to be achieved

VOLUNTEER

Organization 1 • Organization 2 • Organization 3

Milestones to be achieved

HOME MANAGEMENT TASKS

House • Finances • Dogs • Maintenance

Milestones to be achieved

(continued)

Figure 12-2   Individual Planner *(continued)*

WEEKLY PLAN—ENDING M/D/Y

WELLNESS IMPROVEMENT
- Physical   ☐☐ ☐☐ ☐☐ ☐☐
- Mental   ☐☐ ☐☐ ☐☐ ☐
- Spiritual   ☐☐ ☐☐
- Social   ☐☐

FAMILY
Set specific targets and schedule time

WORK ROLE 1
Set specific targets and schedule time

WORK ROLE 2
Set specific targets and schedule time

WORK ROLE 3
Set specific targets and schedule time

VOLUNTEER
Set specific targets and schedule time

HOME
☐ Grocery
☐ Housekeeping
☐ Paperwork
☐ Other

It may help to hire a professional organizer to straighten out your office, kitchen, or garage. Corporations hire efficiency experts for exactly the same reasons.[8]

Another key source of waste that affects individuals' effectiveness is *procrastination*. While it often takes the form of unnecessary human motions, procrastination is generally a "mechanism for coping with the anxiety associated with starting or completing any task or decision."[9] You know what it looks like. So do I.

Why do we procrastinate? Generally, because we are overwhelmed by a task, not because we are lazy. That overwhelming feeling can stem from perfectionism, insecurity, or antipathy for the work to be done. Whatever the case, we perceive that we do not have the time or energy to do what has to be done.

One way to deal with procrastination is by using a work breakdown structure (WBS). For example, I used this approach when writing this book, because I was overwhelmed by the details inherent in pulling it all together. The WBS was helpful in keeping track of the steps for each chapter, things to be researched, diagrams to draft, and publisher's specifications to meet. It helped break things into smaller chunks, so I could still make progress on the manuscript, even if I did not have an entire day to devote to writing. It also mitigated my perfectionist tendencies by breaking "write Chapter 12" into "draft Chapter 12," "revise Chapter 12," and "finalize Chapter 12." This reminded me that the first draft does not have to be perfect.

Ensuring Quality and Continuous Improvement

As noted in Chapter 5, the basic principles for managing quality across an organization are to focus on the customer, promote teamwork and empowerment within the organization, emphasize continuous improvement, identify value added and waste, and reduce variability. This is also true of high-performing individuals. They are effective, in part, because they have the following characteristics:

- They are clear on the desired benefits for their customers.
- They are collaborative and have strong working relationships.
- They always try to do better and learn from experience.

- They are consistent and reliable.
- They work with integrity, and their actions are congruent with their words.

Central to this philosophy is a commitment to continuous improvement, which requires feedback measurement. As we discussed in Chapter 3, a scorecard is a useful measurement system.

YOUR INDIVIDUALIZED SCORECARD

Throughout this book, success has been described in terms of achieving desired results. While the goal of an organization is to make money now and in the future, the desired results for individuals can vary greatly. Some people live to work; others work to live.

Whatever constitutes success for you is up to you—and having specific, measurable goals will help you achieve it. As with a company's balanced scorecard, you may find it appropriate to balance short- and long-term measures, as well as internal (personal) and external (professional) perspectives.

For example, you may envision success as being your own boss, making a difference in others' lives, having financial security, sharing love and laughter with your spouse, and encouraging your children to reach their potential. Each part of this vision can be fulfilled in multiple ways. Being your own boss may mean you own your own business, are a principal in a professional practice, or are self-employed. Making a difference in others' lives can happen in so many ways, such as teaching children, mentoring a disadvantaged person, serving missions, and giving to charity. It is important to translate your vision into specific strategies that you can pursue and measured by goals that indicate your progress.

Let's say you have an exciting idea that you think will allow you to be your own boss, make a difference in others' lives, have financial security, and share love and laughter with your spouse. You want to create a business concept around helping people simplify their lives, work with your spouse to develop a retail presence and consulting methodology, and then franchise the concept around the United States. This might even provide opportunities to cultivate your children's potential. What would a scorecard look like? Initially, it will likely be more of a project plan than a scorecard.

But once you are under way, you might track the kinds of measures listed in Table 12-1.

An individual scorecard may be overly formal for you. However, it may provide a strong sense of self-efficacy, more enjoyment of and engagement with work, better throughput, and better use of your abilities.[10] The point is not so much that you adhere to it religiously, but that you are clear on what is important to you and what you hope to do with your life.

Table 12-1 An Individualized Scorecard Example

Goal	Short-Term Measures	Long-Term Measures	Personal Perspective	Professional Perspective
Be my own boss	Hours per week spent on trivial matters or in reactive mode	Determine timing to hire and franchise	Hours of regular downtime	Hours spent with the local civic club
Make a difference in others' lives	Number of referrals and new clients per month	Number of franchisers, their customers	Hours of volunteer work	Blog weekly; give a speech quarterly
Have financial security	Dollar revenue per month; total net worth	Dollar value of equity in home, savings rate as a percentage of revenue	Tithe each year	Business's debt-to-equity ratio
Share love and laughter	Number of days we start or end the day together	Review retirement plan annually	Have date night each week	Decide on involvement in business
Encourage my children	Hours per week of quality time individually and together	Save for college	Be present for key events	Expose to business each summer

Application and Reflection

1. How do you define personal success for yourself?
2. If you do not have written, measurable goals, try to develop a few.
3. Based on the ideas in this chapter, what top three things could you do to improve your marketability and/or personal effectiveness?

SUMMARY

Parallels between organizational performance and individual effectiveness are grounded in a systems view. They are also related hierarchically; for operations to be managed effectively, processes and projects must be performed effectively, which requires that individuals (particularly managers) perform effectively.

An individual improvement plan should consider the value the individual adds in the workplace and the capabilities he or she has or should have to be successful in a chosen career path. For example, to improve personal effectiveness in the workplace, an individual might invest in further training to develop additional skills, leverage technology to do more with less, and/or control information overload to reduce wasted time. Strong time management and a project view of the individual's workload are also helpful. Reducing waste is also an important consideration.

In addition to increasing productivity, personal effectiveness is based on protecting a person's productive capacity by devoting time to health and well-being. Another element of personal effectiveness is enhancing quality, which comes from being focused on the right things, learning from experience, and working with integrity.

Plans and scorecards are tools that can be used to support an individual's effectiveness.

Review Questions

1. For an individual to be effective, he or she must be part of a high-performing organization.
   a. True
   b. False

2. Which of the following perspectives applies to individual performance?
   a. Systems thinking
   b. Resource-based view
   c. Environmental analysis
   d. a and b
   e. All of the above
3. Which of the following is not an area of focus for individual performance?
   a. Using statistical thinking
   b. Protecting productive capacity
   c. Ensuring quality and continuous improvement
   d. Enhancing individual productivity
4. Which of the following can be sources of waste that detract from individual performance?
   a. Projectizing yourself
   b. Using unnecessary motions
   c. Making mistakes
   d. b and c
   e. All of the above
5. A good way to overcome procrastination is to develop a WBS for the work to be done.
   a. True
   b. False
6. A personal balanced scorecard uses the same areas of performance as those used by a corporation.
   a. True
   b. False

NOTES

CHAPTER 1

1. Meredith, J. R., and S. M. Shaffer. *Operations Management for MBAs, 3/e.* Hoboken, NJ: John Wiley & Sons, 2007.
2. Bustillo, M., and G. A. Fowler. "Wal-Mart Sees Stores as Online Edge." *The Wall Street Journal,* December 15, 2009. Accessed online at http://online.wsj.com.
3. See Wernerfelt, B. "A Resource-Based View of the Firm." *Strategic Management Journal* 5 no. 2 (1984), 171–180, and Wernerfelt, B. "The Resource-Based View of the Firm: Ten Years After." *Strategic Management Journal* 16, no. 3 (1995), 171–174.
4. Kiernan, M. J. "The New Strategic Architecture: Learning to Compete in the Twenty-First Century. *Academy of Management Executive* 7, no. 1 (1993), 7–21.
5. Barney, J. B. "Looking Inside for Competitive Advantage." *Academy of Management Executive* 9, no. 4 (1995), 49–61.
6. Lillis, B., and R. Lane. "Auditing the Strategic Role of Operations." *International Journal of Management Reviews* 9, no. 3 (2007), 191–210.
7. *Business Wire.* "Insight Wins Microsoft Operational Excellence Award: Insight Receives Recognition for the Fifth Time," June 30, 2009. Accessed online at www.cnbc.com.
8. *Business Wire.* "Insight Enterprises Inc. Enters into Definitive Agreement to Acquire Software Spectrum—Accelerating Expansion of Tech-

nology Solutions Capabilities," July 20, 2006. Accessed online at http://findarticles.com.

9. As reported on the company's website and in the *Phoenix Business Journal.* "Insight Enterprises Completes $125M Acquisition of Calence LLC," April 1, 2008, via http://phoenix.bizjournals.com.

CHAPTER 2

1. Porter, M. *Competitive Strategy: Techniques for Analyzing Industries and Competitors.* New York: The Free Press, 1980.
2. Carpenter, M. A., and W. G. Sanders. *Strategic Management: A Dynamic Perspective.* Upper Saddle River, NJ: Prentice Hall, 2008.
3. Atwater, J. B., V. R. Kannan, and A. A. Stephens. "Cultivating Systemic Thinking in the Next Generation of Business Leaders." *Academy of Management Learning & Education* 7, no. 1 (2008), 9–25.
4. Jackson, M. C. *Systems Thinking: Creative Holism for Managers.* New York City: John Wiley & Sons, 2003.
5. Porter, M. E. *Competitive Advantage.* London: The Free Press, 1985.
6. See, for example, Cooper, D. R., and P. S. Schindler. *Business Research Methods, 7/e.* Boston: McGraw-Hill Irwin, 2001, and Davis, D. *Business Research for Decision Making, 5/e.* Pacific Grove, CA: Duxbury Thomas Learning, 2000.
7. Van Aken, J. E., H. Berends, and H. Van der Bij. *Problem-Solving in Organizations: A Methodological Handbook for Business Students.* New York: Cambridge University Press, 2007.
8. Forrester, J. W. "The Counterintuitive Behavior of Social Systems." *Technology Review* 73, no. 3 (1971), 52–68.
9. Senge, P. M. *The Fifth Discipline: The Art & Practice of the Learning Organization.* New York: Doubleday Currency, 1990.
10. Op. cit. Carpenter and Sanders.
11. Op. cit. Porter, 1980.

CHAPTER 3

1. Gerstner, Jr., L. V. *Who Says Elephants Can't Dance? Inside IBM's Historic Turnaround.* New York: HarperCollins Publishers, 2002.
2. Koss, E., and D. A. Lewis. "Productivity or Efficiency—Measuring What We Really Want." *National Productivity Review* 12, no. 2 (1993), 273–284.

3. Crotts, J. C., D. R. Dickson, and R. C. Ford. "Aligning Organizational Processes with Mission: The Case of Service Excellence." *Academy of Management Executive* 19, no. 3 (2005), 54–68.

4. Goleman, D. *Ecological Intelligence: How Knowing the Hidden Impacts of What We Buy Can Change Everything.* New York: Broadway Books, 2009.

5. International Aluminum Institute, "Life Cycle Assessment," http://www.world-aluminium.org/?pg=97.

6. Kaplan, R. S., and D. P. Norton. "Using the Balanced Scorecard as a Strategic Management System." *Harvard Business Review*, (Jan–Feb 1996), 75–85 (reprint #4126).

7. Bendoly, E., E. D. Rosenzweig, and J. K. Stratman. "Performance Metric Portfolios: A Framework and Empirical Analysis." *Production and Operations Management* 16, no. 2 (2007), 257–276.

8. Brown, M. B. "What's Missing from Your Scorecard?" *Balanced Scorecard Report*, May–June 2009.

9. See, for example, Kaplan, R. S., and D. P. Norton. (1996). *The Balanced Scorecard.* Cambridge, MA: Harvard Business School Publishing; Chow, C. W., K. M. Haddad, and J. E. Williamson. "Applying the Balanced Scorecard to Small Companies." *Management Accounting*, (August 1997), 21–27; and Crandall, R. E. "Keys to Better Performance Measures." *IEEE Engineering Management Review* (Second Quarter 2003), 55–60.

10. Schneiderman, A. "Part 3: Selecting Scorecard Metrics." *How to Build a Balanced Scorecard*, 2006. Accessed online at http://www.schneiderman.com.

11. Op. cit. Brown.

12. Likierman, A. "The Five Traps of Performance Measurement." *Harvard Business Review*, October 2009, 96–101 (reprint R0910L).

CHAPTER 4

1. Abrahamson, E. "Change Without Pain." *Harvard Business Review*, July/August 2000, reprint #R00401. Accessed online at http://hbswk.hbs.edu/archive/1683.html.

2. Wheelwright, S. C., and K. B. Clark. "Creating Project Plans to Focus Product Development." *Harvard Business Review*, March–April 1992, 70–82, reprint 92210.

3. Christensen, C. M., and M. E. Raynor. *The Innovator's Solution*. Boston: Harvard Business School Press, 2003.

4. Immelt, J. R., V. Govindarajan, and C. Trimble. "How GE Is Disrupting Itself." *Harvard Business Review* October 2009, 56–65. Reprint R0910D.

5. Christiansen, C. M. *The Innovator's Dilemma: The Revolutionary Book That Will Change the Way You Do Business*. New York: Collins Business Essentials, 2003.

6. Ferrin, B. G., and R. E. Plan. "Total Cost of Ownership Models: An Exploratory Study." *Journal of Supply Chain Management* 38, no. 3 (2002), 18–29.

7. Schmenner, R. W. "How Can Service Businesses Survive and Prosper?" *Sloan Management Review* 27, no. 3 (1986), 21–32.

8. Brennan, L. L. "Operations Management for Engineering Consulting Firms: A Case Study." *Journal of Management in Engineering* 2, no. 3 (2006), 98–107.

9. Goetsch, D. L., and S. B. Davis. *Quality Management: Introduction to Total Quality Management for Production, Processing & Services*. Upper Saddle River, NJ: Prentice Hall, 2000.

CHAPTER 5

1. Hardie, T. "The Effects of Quality on Business Performance." *Quality Management Journal* 5, no. 3 (1998), 59–59.

2. Meredith, J. R., and S. M. Shaffer. Operations *Management for MBAs, 3/e*. Hoboken: John Wiley & Sons, 2007, pp. 137–138.

3. Walton, M. *The Deming Management Method*. New York: Putnam Publishing, 1986.

4. Anderson, J. C., M. Rungstusanatham, and R. G. Schroeder. "A Theory of Quality Management Underlying the Deming Management Method." *Academy of Management Review* 19, no. 3 (1994), 472–509.

5. Juran, J. M. *Juran on Planning for Quality*. New York City: The Free Press, 1988.

6. Crosby, P. B. *Quality Is Free*. New York City: Penguin Books, 1980.

7. Ireland, L. R. *Quality Management for Projects and Programs*. Sylva, NC: Project Management Institute, 1991.

8. Terlap, S., and K. Linebaugh. "Toyota Says It Fixed 500,000 Vehicles." *The Wall Street Journal*, February 15, 2010. Accessed online at http://online.wsj.com on February 19, 2010.

9. Zhang, J. "Cookie Dough Is Linked to E. Coli Risks." *The Wall Street Journal*, June 20, 2009. Accessed online at http://online.wsj.com on September 2, 2009.

10. Dean, Jr., J. W., and D. E. Bowen. "Management Theory and Total Quality: Improving Research and Practice through Theory Development." *Academy of Management Review* 19, no. 3 (1994), 392–418.

11. Ibid.

12. Op. cit. Hardie.

13. Wisner, J. D., and S. G. Eakins. "A Performance Assessment of the US Baldrige Quality Award Winners." *International Journal of Quality & Reliability Management* 11, no. 2 (1997), 8–25.

14. Skrabec Jr., Q. R., T. S. Ragu-Nathan, S. S. Rao, and B. T. Bhatt. "ISO 9000: Do the Benefits Outweigh the Costs?" *Industrial Management* (November/December 1997), 26–32.

15. Goetsch, D. L., and S. B. Davis. *Understanding and Implementing ISO 9000 and ISO Standards.* Upper Saddle River, NJ: Prentice-Hall, 1998.

16. Snee, R. D., and R. W. Hoerl. *Leading Six Sigma.* Upper Saddle River, NJ: Prentice Hall, 2003.

17. Op. cit. Meredith and Shaeffer.

18. Liker, J., and D. Meier. *The Toyota Way Fieldbook.* New York City: McGraw-Hill, 2005.

19. Chase, R. B., and D. M. Stewart. "Make Your Service Fail-Safe." *Sloan Management Review* 35, no. 3 (1994), 35–44 (reprint 3533).

20. Landro, L. "Catching Deadly Drug Mistakes." *The Wall Street Journal*, January 18, 2010. Accessed online at http://online.wsj.com on February 5, 2010.

21. Op. cit. Chase and Stewart, p. 37.

22. daCosta, C. "Video Game Urinal." *Gadget Review*, March 22, 2006. Accessed online at http://www.gadgetreview.com/20006/03/video-game-urinal.html .

23. Gawande, A. *The Checklist Manifesto: How to Get Things Right.* New York City: Metropolitan Books, 2009.

24. Op. cit. Snee and Hoerl.

25. Op. cit. Ireland, 1991, p. IV-7.

CHAPTER 6

1. Kelly, K. *New Rules for the New Economy: 10 Radical Strategies for a Connected World.* New York City: Penguin USA, 1999.

2. Microsoft. "MediaCart, Microsoft and Wakefern Team Up to Deliver Next-Generation Digital Grocery Shopping and Ad Experience." Company press release, January 14, 2008. Accessed online at www.microsoft.com.

3. Department of Energy. *The Smart Grid: An Introduction.* Available online at www.oe.energy.gov/SmartGridIntroduction.htm.

4. Brennan, L. L. "Pervasive or Invasive? A Strategic Approach to IT-Enabled Access and Immediacy." *Journal of Organizational and End User Computing* 21, no. 4 (2009), 63–72.

5. Owen, J. *The Death of Modern Management: How to Lead in the New World Disorder.* West Sussex, UK: John Wiley & Sons, 2009.

6. Sproull, L., and S. Kiesler. *Connections: New Ways of Working in the Networked Organization.* Cambridge: MIT Press, 1992.

7. Davenport, T., and J. Short. "The New Industrial Engineering: Information Technology and Business Process Redesign." *Sloan Management Review,* (Summer 1990), 11–27.

8. Karmi, J. "What Are the Key Attributes of Supply Chain Management (SCM) Systems?" In Laube, D. R., and Zammuto, eds. *Business Driven Information Technology: Answers to 100 Critical Questions for Every Manager.* Palo Alto, CA: Stanford University Press, 1990.

9. Scott, J. "What Risks Does an Organization Face from an ERP Implementation?" In Laube, D. R., and Zammuto, eds. *Business Driven Information Technology: Answers to 100 Critical Questions for Every Manager.* Palo Alto, CA: Stanford University Press, 1990.

10. IT Cortex. "Failure Rate: Statistics over IT Project Failure Rates," 2009. Accessed online at www.it-cortex.com/Stat_Failure_Rate.htm.

11. Anderson, B. "What are the Attributes of a Good CRM System?" In Laube, D. R., and Zammuto, eds. *Business Driven Information Technology: Answers to 100 Critical Questions for Every Manager.* Palo Alto, CA: Stanford University Press, 1990.

12. Tyler, J. "Devil Shoppers." Broadcast on *National Public Radio,* December 11, 2004, American Public Media. Accessed online at http://marketplace.publicradio.org.

13. Shih, C. *The Facebook Era: Tapping Online Social Networks to Build Better Products, Reach New Audiences, and Sell More Stuff.* Upper Saddle, NJ: Prentice-Hall, 2009.

14. Ibid, p. 66.

15. Wreden, N. "The Promise of 'Self-Segmentation." *Strategy + Business* October 5, 2009. Available online at www.strategy-business.com.

16. Shroeder, S. "The Web in Numbers: The Rise of Social Media." *Mashable: The Social Media Guide* April 17, 2009. Available online at http://mashable.com.

17. Walczak, W., and C. M. Fiol. "What Is 'Knowledge Management?'" In Laube, D. R., and Zammuto, eds. *Business Driven Information Technology: Answers to 100 Critical Questions for Every Manager.* Palo Alto, CA: Stanford University Press, 1990.

18. Huber, G. P. "Organizational Learning: The Contributing Processes and the Literatures." *Organization Science* 2, no. 1 (1991), 88–115.

19. Op. cit. Owen, p. 153.

20. Tapscott, D., and A. D. Williams. *Wikinomics: How Mass Collaboration Changes Everything.* New York City: Penguin Group, 2008.

21. Ibid, p. 107.

22. Orlikowski, W. J. "The Sociomateriality of Organizational Life: Considering Technology in Management Research." *Cambridge Journal of Economics* (2010), 125–141.

23. Yourdon, E. *Death March: The Complete Software Developer's Guide to Surviving "Mission Impossible" Projects.* Upper Saddle River, NJ: Prentice Hall, 1997.

24. Steele, L. *Managing Technology: The Strategic View.* New York City: McGraw-Hill, 1989.

25. Curtis, B., W. E. Hefley, and S. A. Miller. *The People CMM: A Framework for Human Capital Management, 2/e.* Canada: Addison-Wesley Professional, 2009.

26. Software Engineering Institute. "People Capability Maturity Model—Version 2." Accessed online at www.sei.cmu.edu.

28. Lewis, C. "How Can the Capability Maturity Model (CMM) Be Used to Improve an IT Organization's Effectiveness?" In Laube, D. R., and Zammuto, eds. *Business Driven Information Technology: Answers to 100 Critical Questions for Every Manager.* Palo Alto, CA: Stanford University Press, 2003.

CHAPTER 7

1. Op. cit. Porter, 1985.

2. Op. cit. Davenport and Short, p. 12.

3. Leonard, J., and A. E. Grey. "Process Fundamentals." *Harvard Business School Teaching Notes*. Boston: Harvard Business School Press, 1995 (Reprint 9-696-023).

4. Prahalad, C. K., and M. S. Krishnan. *The New Age of Innovation: Driving Cocreated Value Through Global Networks*. New York City: McGraw-Hill, 2008.

5. Klassen, R. D., and L. J. Menor. "The Process Management Triangle: An Empirical Investigation of Process Trade-Offs." *Journal of Operations Management* 25 (2007), 1015–1034.

6. Metters, R., and V. Vargas. "Organizing Work in Service Firms." *Business Horizons* (July–August 2000), 23–32.

7. Hammer, M., and J. Champy. *Reengineering the Corporation: A Manifesto for Business Revolution*. New York City: HarperBusiness, 1993.

8. Klein, M. "The Most Fatal Reengineering Mistakes." *Information Strategy: The Executive's Journal* (Summer 1994), 21–28.

9. Goldratt, E. M., and J. Cox. *The Goal: A Process of Ongoing Improvement, 3/e*. Great Barrington, MA: North River Press, 1994.

10. Sheinkopf, L. J. *Thinking for a Change: Putting the TOC Thinking Processes to Use*. Boca Raton, FL: St. Lucie Press, 1999.

11. Burton-Houle, T. *The Theory of Constraints and Its Thinking Processes*. New Haven, CT: The Goldratt Institute, 2001.

12. Ibid.

13. Passariello, C. "In France, a Drive-Up Grocery Takes Off." *The Wall Street Journal*, January 14, 2010. Accessed online at http://online.wsj.com on February 5, 2010.

14. Few, S. C. *Now You See It: Simple Visualization Techniques for Quantitative Analysis*. Oakland, CA: Analytics Press, 2010.

CHAPTER 8

1. McClave, J. T., P. G. Benson, and T. Sincich. *Statistics for Business and Economics, 3/e*. Upper Saddle River, NJ: Prentice Hall, 2008.

2. Ibid, p. 795.

3. Turner, L., and R. Turner. "Chapter 1: How to Recognize When Special Causes Exist." *A Guide to Statistical Process Control*. Ends of the

Earth Learning Group. Accessed online at http://www.endsoftheearth .com/SPC/Chap1.htm.

4. Op. cit. McClave et al.

5. Hare, L. B., R. W. Hoerl, J. D. Hromi, and R. D. Snee. "The Role of Statistical Thinking in Management." *The ASQ.* Reprinted in *IEEE Engineering Management Review* (Fall 1998), 69–77.

6. Francis, V. E. "Winning Hearts and Minds: An Argument for Quantitative Management in an Operations Management Course." *Decision Sciences Journal of Innovative Education* 7, no. 1 (January 2009): 73–79.

7. Krajewski, L. J, L. P. Ritzman, and M. K. Malhotra. *Operations Management: Processes and Supply Chains, 9/e.* Upper Saddle River, NJ: Prentice Hall.

CHAPTER 9

1. Pinto, J. K., and O. P. Kharbanda. "Lessons for an Accidental Profession." *Business Horizons* 38, no. 2 (1995), 41–50. Reprinted in *Engineering Management Review* 23, no. 4 (1996), 18–27.

2. Project Management Institute. *A Guide to the Project Management Body of Knowledge (PMBOK® Guide): 3/e.* Newtown Square: Project Management Institute, 2004.

3. See, for example, Jang, J., G. Klein, and J. Balloun. "Ranking System Implementation Success Factors." *Project Management Journal,* December 1996, 49–53.

4. Gido, J., and J. P. Clements. *Successful Project Management, 2/e.* Mason, OH: Thompson South-Western, 2003.

5. Orwig, R. A., and L. L. Brennan. "An Integrated View of Project and Quality Management for Project-based Organizations." *International Journal of Quality & Reliability Management* 17, no. 4/5 (2000), 351–363.

6. Bailey, A. "Uh-Oh. It's a Computer Systems Project . . ." *IEEE Engineering Management Review* (winter 1998), 21–25.

7. Goldratt, E. M. *The Critical Chain.* Great Barrington, MA: North River Press, 1996.

CHAPTER 10

1. Raz, T., and S. Globerson. "Effective Sizing and Content Definition of Work Packages." *Project Management Journal* 29, no. 4 (December 1998), 17–23.
2. Op. cit. Goldratt.
3. Nevison, J. "Up to Speed: The Cost of Learning on a White-Collar Project." *Project Management Journal*, June 1994, 45–49.

CHAPTER 11

1. Brennan, L. L., and W. W. Austin. "Addressing the Need for Management Processes in Higher Education Accreditation." *Innovative Higher Education* 28, no. 1 (fall 2003), 49–62.
2. Mantel, Jr., S. J., J. R. Meredith, S. M. Shafer, and M. M. Sutton. *Project Management in Practice*. New York City: John Wiley & Sons, 2001.
3. Pinto, J. "Twelve Ways to Get the Least from Yourself and Your Project." *PM Network* (May 1997), 29–31, with permission.
4. Baker, B. "Great Expectations: Turning Failure Into Success—and Vice Versa." *PM Network* (May 1997), 25–28.
5. Lippincott, S. *Meetings: Do's, Don'ts and Donuts*. Pittsburgh: Lighthouse Point Press, 1994.
6. Doyle, M., and D. Straus. *How to Make Meetings Work: The New Interaction Method*. New York City: Berkley Books, 1993.

CHAPTER 12

1. Covey, S. R. "Use Your Voice of Influence." *Success from Home* 2, no. 10 (2006), 513. Pinto, J. "Twelve Ways to Get the Least from Yourself and Your Project." *PM Network* (May 1997), 29–31, with permission.
2. Covey, S. R. *The 7 Habits of Highly Effective People*. New York City: The Free Press, 2004.
3. Perlow, L. A., and J. L. Porter. "Making Time off Predictable—& Required." *Harvard Business Review* (October 2009), 1023. Pinto, J. "Twelve Ways to Get the Least from Yourself and Your Project." *PM Network* (May 1997), 29–31, with permission. 109 (reprint R0910M).
4. Crovitz, L. G. "Unloading Information Overload." *The Wall Street Journal*, July 7, 2008. Accessed online at http://online.wsj.com.
5. Op. cit. Covey, 2004.

6. Peters, T. *The Circle of Innovation: You Can't Shrink Your Way to Greatness*. New York City: Alfred A. Knopf, 1997.

7. Maxwell, J. C. *Thinking for a Change: 11 Ways Highly Successful People Approach Life and Work*. Nashville: Center Street, 2005.

8. Kestenbaum, D. "Do You Waste Time Walking to the Printer?" Broadcast on *National Public Radio*, February 18, 2010. Accessed online at npr.org.

9. Fiore, N. *The Now Habit: A Strategic Program for Overcoming Procrastination and Enjoying Guilt-Free Play*. New York City: Jeremy P. Tarcher/Penguin, 2007.

10. Rampersad, H. K. *Personal Balance Scorecard: The Way to Individual Happiness, Personal Integrity, and Organizational Effectiveness*. Greenwich, CT: Information Age Publishing, 2006.

INDEX

INSTRUCTIONS FOR ACCESSING ONLINE FINAL EXAM AND CHAPTER QUIZ ANSWERS

I f you have completed your study of *The McGraw-Hill 36-Hour Course: Operations Management,* you should be prepared to take the online final examination. It is a comprehensive test, consisting of 100 multiple-choice questions. You may treat this test as an "open book" exam by consulting this book and any other resources. Answers to both the online exam and the chapter-ending quizzes can be found on The McGraw-Hill 36-Hour Course Information Center landing site for each book (please see the instructions below for accessing the site).

Instructions for Accessing Online Final Exam
1. Go to www.36hourbooks.com.
2. Once you arrive on the home page, scroll down until you find The McGraw-Hill 36-Hour Course: Operations Management and click

the link "Test your skills here." At this point you will be redirected to The McGraw-Hill 36-Hour Course Information Center landing site for the book.

3. Click the "Click Here to Begin" button in the center of the landing site. You will be brought to a page containing detailed instructions for taking the final exam and obtaining your Certificate of Achievement.

4. Click on "Self-Assessment Quiz" in the left-hand navigation bar to begin the exam.

Instructions for Accessing Answers to Chapter-Ending Quizzes

1. Follow Steps 1 and 2 above.

2. Click "Chapter-Ending Quiz Answers" in the left-hand navigation bar.

ABOUT THE AUTHOR

Linda L. Brennan, Ph.D., is a professor of management at Mercer University in Macon, Georgia. Her teaching portfolio includes graduate and undergraduate courses in operations management, leadership, international business, and strategy. She also conducts research and consults in the areas of technology impact assessment, process and project management, and instructional effectiveness for a wide variety of organizations, including Fortune 100 companies, professional services firms, and many not-for-profit organizations. Dr. Brennan's prior work experience includes management positions at The Quaker Oats Company and marketing and systems engineering experience with the IBM Corporation. A licensed professional engineer, she received her Ph.D. in industrial engineering from Northwestern University, her M.B.A. in policy studies from the University of Chicago, and her B.I.E. in industrial engineering from the Georgia Institute of Technology. She lives in Central Georgia with her husband, teenage son, dog, and cat.

R.C.L.

AVR. 2011

A